Great Meals in Minutes was created by Rebus, Inc. and published by Time-Life Books.

Rebus, Inc.

Publisher: Rodney Friedman
Editor: Shirley Tomkievicz
Executive Editor: Marya Dalrymple
Art Director: Ronald Gross
Managing Editor: Brenda Goldberg
Senior Editor: Cara De Silva
Food Editor and Food Stylist: Grace Young
Photographer: Steven Mays
Prop Stylist: Cathryn Schwing
Staff Writer: Alexandra Greeley
Associate Editor: Jordan Verner
Editorial Assistant: Bonnie J. Slotnick
Assistant Food Stylist: Nancy Leland Thompson
Recipe Tester: Gina Palombi Barclay
Production Assistant: Lorna Bieber

For information about any Time-Life book, please write:
Reader Information
Time-Life Books
541 North Fairbanks Court
Chicago, Illinois 60611

Library of Congress Cataloging in Publication Data
Mexican menus.
      (Great meals in minutes)
      Includes index.
      1. Cookery, Mexican.   2. Menus.
      3. Cooks—Biography
I. Time-Life Books.   II. Series.
TX716.M4M5   1984   641.5972   84-8867
ISBN 0-86706-187-1 (lib. bdg.)
ISBN 0-86706-186-3 (retail ed.)

Time-Life Books Inc.
is a wholly owned subsidiary of
Time Incorporated
Founder: Henry R. Luce 1898–1967
Editor-in-Chief: Henry Anatole Grunwald
President: J. Richard Munro
Chairman of the Board: Ralph P. Davidson
Corporate Editor: Jason McManus
Group Vice President, Books: Joan D. Manley

Time-Life Books Inc.

Editor: George Constable
Executive Editor: George Daniels
Director of Design: Louis Klein
Board of Editors: Dale M. Brown, Thomas A. Lewis, Robert G. Mason, Ellen Phillips, Peter Pocock, Gerry Schremp, Gerald Simons, Rosalind Stubenberg, Kit van Tulleken, Henry Woodhead
Director of Administration: David L. Harrison
Director of Research: Carolyn L. Sackett
Director of Photography: John Conrad Weiser

President: Reginald K. Brack Jr.
Senior Vice President: William Henry
Vice Presidents: George Artandi, Stephen L. Bair, Robert A. Ellis, Juanita T. James, Christopher T. Linen, James L. Mercer, Joanne A. Pello, Paul R. Stewart

Editorial Operations
Design: Anne B. Landry (art coordinator); James J. Cox (quality control)
Research: Phyllis K. Wise (assistant director), Louise D. Forstall
Copy Room: Diane Ullius
Production: Celia Beattie, Gordon E. Buck,
Correspondent: Miriam Hsia (New York)

SERIES CONSULTANT
Margaret E. Happel is the author of *Ladies Home Journal Adventures in Cooking, Ladies Home Journal Handbook of Holiday Cuisine,* and other best-selling cookbooks, as well as the translator and adapter of Rebecca Hsu Hiu Min's *Delights of Chinese Cooking.* A food consultant based in New York City, she has been director of the food department of *Good Housekeeping* and editor of *American Home* magazine.

WINE CONSULTANT
Tom Maresca combines a full-time career teaching English literature with writing about and consuming fine wines. He is now at work on *The Wine Case Book,* which explains the techniques of wine tasting.

Cover: Lucinda Hutson's marinated red snapper and citrus salad with pomegranate seeds. See pages 84–85.

Great Meals
IN MINUTES

MEXICAN
MENUS

TIME-LIFE BOOKS, ALEXANDRIA, VIRGINIA

Contents

Meet the Cooks

JANE BUTEL

Born and raised in New Mexico, Jane Butel grew up eating such native foods as Navajo fry bread and blue-corn tortillas. Before moving to Manhattan to head the Pecos Valley Spice Company, which sells ingredients for Mexican meals, she worked as a home economist in New Mexico. She is the author of five Mexican cookbooks, including *Favorite Mexican Foods*, *Chili Madness*, and *Jane Butel's Tex-Mex Cookbook*.

ELIZABETH SCHNEIDER

Elizabeth Schneider has been a New York-based food journalist for a dozen years, writing regularly for *Food & Wine* and a number of other magazines. She is also the author of *Ready When You Are: Made-Ahead Meals for Entertaining* and the coauthor of *Better Than Store-Bought*, which won a Tastemaker Award in 1979. She was a contributor to both *The Cooks' Catalog* and *The International Cooks' Catalog*.

SUE HUFFMAN

Sue Huffman, food and equipment editor of *Ladies' Home Journal*, began her culinary career as food editor of the *St. Louis Globe Democrat*. A member of Les Dames d'Escoffier (an honorary society for women in the food professions) and the New York Women's Culinary Alliance, she is the mother of two teenagers who serve as tasters for her experiments in the kitchen.

BARBARA HANSEN

As a food writer for the *Los Angeles Times*, Barbara Hansen initiated a regular cooking column on Mexican cuisine, called "Border Line." She has taught Mexican cooking at the University of California, Los Angeles, extension school and gives lectures about and demonstrations of Mexican cooking. She is the author of *Cooking California Style*, *Good Bread*, and, most recently, *Mexican Cookery*.

RICK BAYLESS

Rick Bayless learned traditional southwestern cooking at his family's barbecue restaurant in Oklahoma. After college he lived in Mexico and developed a passion for Mexican food. Besides having created a television series, "Cooking Mexican with Rick Bayless," he has been a caterer, cooking instructor, chef, and restaurant consultant. He is writing a book on regional Mexican cookery.

CONSTANTINE COULES

Constantine Coules began his food career in New York as a student of several master chefs and later ran his own free-lance catering firm. His travels throughout Europe, the United States, and Mexico inspire his recipes. He is currently writing a cookbook and preparing a series of video-cassette cooking lessons.

VICKIE SIMMS

Vickie Simms, a native Californian who now lives in San Francisco, specializes in recipe development and food styling for television commercials and other advertising. Initially trained as a French cook, she has also studied the cuisines of Italy, China, California, and Mexico. She learned about Mexican food while living for six years in a Mexican community in Los Angeles.

LUCINDA HUTSON

Lucinda Hutson has traveled extensively in Mexico interviewing regional cooks. For the past ten years she has taught classes in traditional Mexican recipes and techniques—and her own style of Mexican cooking—in Austin, Texas. Her extensive herb garden yields many Mexican herbs.

MARGARET SHAKESPEARE

Margaret Shakespeare, a New York-based writer, began her career as a caterer for after-theater parties. She then went into recipe development and menu design, specializing in the adaptation of ethnic recipes for American home cooks. She has written about food, travel, and culture for *Gourmet*, *The COOK'S Magazine*, the *New York Times*, and *Connoisseur*; she is also the author of *The Meringue Cookbook* and *California: Land of Many Dreams*.

Mexican Menus in Minutes

GREAT MEALS FOR FOUR IN AN HOUR OR LESS

To many Americans, Mexican food means a taco—chicken, beef, or cheese wrapped in a tortilla—or a fiery bowl of *chili con carne*, which probably is not even a Mexican creation. But Mexican food is infinitely more diverse, as simple as the familiar Indian *tamales* (cornmeal dough with a sweet or savory filling baked in corn husks) or as elegant as the national dish, *mole poblano* (a chili-and-chocolate-based turkey stew, said to have been created by sixteenth-century Spanish nuns in Mexico). Mexican cooking, with all its complex and exotic flavors, ranks with French, Chinese, and Italian cuisines as one of the most sophisticated in the world.

The cuisine of Mexico owes its extraordinary diversity to a blending of two cultures. When Cortés and his Spanish soldiers marched into the Aztec capital of Tenochtitlán (now Mexico City) in 1519, they were dazzled by a strange Indian civilization. The Aztecs, a fierce, once-nomadic tribe that had settled in the central Mexico valley in the 1300s, had become a powerful political force, conquering many lesser tribes and ruling much of the land. They had also developed a complex society, renowned for its architectural, commercial, and cultural achievements.

The Spaniards were equally capitivated by the Indians' sumptuous cuisine, concocted from ingredients carried into the the capital from every part of Mexico. In his journals, the Spanish soldier Bernal Díaz del Castillo made note of the Aztec diet, all foods hitherto unknown to Europeans: corn, beans, squash, peanuts, chocolate, avocados, turkey, tomatoes, vanilla, eggplant, and chilies. His compatriot, Friar Bernardino de Sahagún, also wrote about the meals of the Aztec nobles, with their corn flour flatbreads, frothy chocolate drinks, roast quail and turkey, red tamales with beans, and small cactus fruits.

Peasant cooking at the time was as varied as the Indian cultures from which it developed. Corn, beans, squash, and chilies were the cornerstone of the peasant diet. Of these, corn was the most important and most venerated. Aztec mythology describes the introduction of corn by the great god Quetzalcóatl, who turned himself into an ant in order to steal corn for the newly created human race. The sacred Mayan book *Popul Vuh* includes another creation myth in which four men and four women were made from the doughs of white and yellow maize. No wonder that the grain was, and is, the basis of so many national and regional dishes and that thrifty Mexicans have some use for every part of the corn plant. Additionally, rich sauces, or *moles* (from the Aztec word *molli*, meaning sauce flavored with chili) characterized the food. Moles are chili-based and vary from region to region; the mole poblano is just one version of this Indian invention.

The Spaniards gradually assimilated these novel foods, but the culinary exchange was not one-sided. The conquistadores contributed much to the Indian larders: wine, hogs, cattle, chickens, onions, garlic, citrus fruits, almonds, dairy products, cinnamon, olive oil, rice, and wheat. Spanish cooks also taught the Aztecs how to fry foods. Previously, they had cooked on dry griddles. This transformed the cuisine, since probably half of all Mexican foods are now fried rather than baked or boiled. Today's Mexican food, still a mix of Indian and Spanish, also reflects other European influences, including French, Austrian, and Italian (all introduced during the brief rule of the French Empire from 1864 to 1867).

To the uninitiated, Mexican food and its Tex-Mex offshoots may seem esoteric and chili-laden, but most people, once they have tasted a good Mexican meal, quickly become devotees. In fact, Mexican cooking grows more popular with Americans each year.

On the following pages, nine of America's most talented cooks present 27 complete menus featuring Mexican and Mexican-American meals. Every menu can be made in an hour or less. They use fresh produce, with no powdered sauces or other dubious shortcuts. Additional ingredients (vinegars, spices, herbs, and so on) are all high quality yet available, for the most part, in supermarkets or, occasionally, in specialty shops. Each of the menus serves four people.

The photographs accompanying each meal show exactly how the dishes will look when you bring them to the table. The cooks and the test kitchen have planned the meals for appearance as well as taste: The vegetables are brilliant and fresh, the visual combinations appetizing. The table settings feature bright colors, simple flower arrange-

A red snapper, raw shrimp, a chicken breast, radishes, and a tomato on a bed of lettuce and coriander, opposite, await preparation for a Mexican meal. Arranged on the terra-cotta tiles as well is a grouping of provisions Mexican cooks would stock (clockwise, from top left): tostaditas, *yellow cornmeal and* masa harina, *red* salsa cruda, *dried oregano, corn tortillas, tropical fruits, cinnamon sticks, golden raisins, solid Mexican chocolate, three varieties of chili powder, fresh and dried whole chilies, a red pepper,* tomatillos, *pine nuts and pumpkin seeds, and grated Monterey Jack cheese.*

ments, and attractive, but not necessarily expensive, serving pieces. You can readily adapt your own tableware to these menus in convenient ways that will please you and your guests.

For each menu, the Editors, with advice from the cooks, suggest wines and other beverages. And there are suggestions for the best uses of leftovers and for appropriate side dishes and desserts. You will find a range of other tips, too, on the best ways to select and prepare fresh produce. All the recipes have been tested meticulously to make sure that even a relatively inexperienced cook can complete them within the time limit.

BEFORE YOU START

Great Meals in Minutes is designed for efficiency and ease. This book will work best for you if you follow these suggestions:

1. Read the guidelines (pages 9–13) for selecting Mexican ingredients.

2. Refresh your memory with the few simple cooking techniques on the following pages. They will quickly become second nature and will help you produce professional meals in minutes.

3. Read the menus before you shop. Each one opens with a list of all the ingredients, in the order you would expect to shop for them in the average supermarket. Check for those few you need to buy; many items will already be on your pantry shelf.

4. Check the equipment list on page 14. A good, sharp knife or knives and pots and pans of the right shape and material are essential for making great meals in minutes. This may be the time to look critically at what you own and to plan to buy a few things. The right equipment can turn cooking from a necessity into a creative experience.

5. Get out everything you need before you start to cook: The lists at the beginning of each menu tell just what is required. To save effort, keep your equipment and ingredients close at hand and always put them in the same place so you can reach for them instinctively.

6. Take your meat, fish, and dairy products out of the refrigerator early enough for them to come to room temperature and thereby cut cooking time.

7. Follow the start-to-finish steps for each menu. That way, you can be sure of having the entire meal ready to serve at the right moment.

REGIONAL STYLES OF MEXICAN COOKING

Certain dishes, with minor variations, are standard throughout Mexico. Some familiar examples include *tortillas* (flat, unleavened bread made from cornmeal or wheat flour), *tacos* (a variety of fillings wrapped in tortillas), *guacamole* (seasoned mashed avocado served as a dip or a sauce), *enchiladas* (filled tortillas baked in a sauce), custards, chicken soups, and refried beans. But for the most part, Mexican cooking varies considerably from region to region, largely because of topography and climate. Modern communications and superhighways have helped to break down some of this regional insularity, and

people in the north are now able to sample such Yucatecan dishes as chicken *en escabeche* (chicken in a "pickling" sauce) and puréed black beans. Americans have created their own regional versions of Mexican cooking, altering traditional Mexican recipes to suit their own ingredients and tastes.

South of the Border

Mexico can be divided into several broad areas, each with its own distinctive cooking styles and dishes based on the ingredients indigenous to the region. For instance, in the arid north—cattle and wheat country—dried beef, cheese-based dishes, wheat tortillas, and barbecued foods abound.

Central Mexico, where the Aztecs thrived and developed their corn-based cuisine, features tamales and enchiladas. Tortilla-based casseroles, freshwater fish and seafood, pork, goat, chicken, and venison take the place of beef. Examples of local dishes are the *pozole* (hominy) of Jalisco, the *chiles en nogada* (chilies in nut sauce) of Puebla, and red snapper Veracruz-style.

The most distinctive of all Mexican regional foods comes from the Yucatan, the southeastern peninsula noted for its tropical fruits, seafood, and meat and fowl dishes called *pibil* (in which the food is rubbed with a seasoning paste, wrapped in banana leaves, then steamed in a pit). See Rick Bayless (pages 54–63) for foods in the Yucatecan style.

North of the Border

Mexican-American cooking is an amalgam of foods handed down by Spanish and other European settlers, Mexican immigrants, and American Indians. It differs from state to state in the southwest and west.

Tex-Mex cooking, with its roots in northern Mexico-style cooking, is generally characterized by the plentiful use of fresh and dried chilies, tortillas, barbecued meats, cheeses, tacos, and tamales. Texas cooks also take credit for inventing the first bowl of chili—cubes of beef in a spicy sauce. Jane Butel's Chili with No Beans (page 25) is an example of Tex-Mex cooking.

In New Mexico, the cuisine (also called Santa-Fe style) is more Spanish and Indian than Mexican and has strong peasant roots. It is simpler and less fatty than Tex-Mex, featuring puffy breads, wild greens, a preponderance of chilies, and products made from the unique variety of blue corn indigenous to New Mexico. Elizabeth Schneider's recipe for Green Chili and Cheese Enchiladas (page 32) is representative of this type of cooking.

Arizona's Mexican foods have deep Indian roots. Cooks there make use of such ingredients as cactus, beef jerky, mild green chilies, large wheat tortillas, beans, and rice.

Californians have produced an eclectic, more refined Mexican cuisine, known as Cal-Mex, reminiscent of Italian and Oriental cooking. Fresh fruits and vegetables, seafood, mild chili sauces, and coriander predominate.

MEXICAN INGREDIENTS

If you are cooking Mexican food for the first time, you will be surprised to find that most of the ingredients needed—

such as corn and wheat tortillas, chilies, and beans—are in your supermarket. Indeed, many of the recipes in this volume can be prepared from ingredients you already have on your pantry shelf. If your supermarket does not stock fresh chilies or pure chili powders, you can find them at Mexican or Spanish groceries or at food shops that specialize in ethnic foods. You can also order these items by mail: See page 103 for a list of mail-order sources for Mexican ingredients.

Chilies

There are at least 100 varieties of chilies grown in Mexico (and nearly as many "expert" opinions about their classification). Only a few of these varieties are available—fresh, dried, or canned—in some parts of the United States. For this reason, the cooks in this volume or the Editors frequently suggest substitutes for chilies called for in the recipes.

Large fresh chilies tend to be more flavorful but less fiery than the small dried ones. Most of the heat comes from the chili seeds and interior membranes, or ribs, which you can remove and discard for milder flavor. In general, the smaller the chili, the hotter it is.

Use large fresh chilies for sauces and as major ingredients in special dishes such as stuffed chilies; use small fresh chilies for garnishes and relishes. Use dried chilies, small or large, for sauces or for grinding into chili powders. Several varieties of fresh chilies come canned—the Anaheim (usually labeled only "mild, green"), the *jalapeño*, and the *serrano* among them.

Many chilies have different regional names, and, to add to the confusion, a fresh chili may have one name and its dried form another—for instance, a dried *poblano* is an *ancho*. Your best bet is to try several different varieties in your cooking, then select those that suit you. Be warned, however, that "hotness" varies with the season and growing conditions, so that chilies of the same name (or even the same plant) will not always be of the same hotness.

FRESH CHILIES

The menus in this volume call for four kinds of fresh chilies:

Anaheim: Also known as California green chilies, these bright green pods are 5 to 7 inches long and are usually very mild. (A similar variety grown in Mexico is hotter.) They have firm, thick flesh and are abundant in the west and southwest. Elsewhere, check Mexican groceries.

Serrano: These very small (about 1½ inches long and ½ inch wide) chilies are available in areas with large Mexican communities, but otherwise are hard to find. You can substitute jalapeños.

Poblano: Triangular and about 4½ inches long and 2½ inches wide, these chilies are dark green and variably hot. They are not widely available, except in groceries in Mexican communities. Allowing for subtle differences in flavor and hotness, you can use poblano and Anaheim chilies interchangeably.

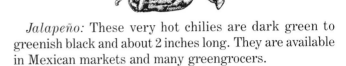

Jalapeño: These very hot chilies are dark green to greenish black and about 2 inches long. They are available in Mexican markets and many greengrocers.

When you buy fresh chilies, select those that are firm, plump, and smooth. Their skins should be shiny and unblemished. Whole chilies will keep, refrigerated, for up to two weeks if wrapped in paper towels and then placed in a paper bag. They should never be tightly wrapped in plastic, as moisture causes them to decay. They will keep, frozen, up to a year if they are preboiled or roasted.

A number of the recipes in this book call for roasting fresh chilies, which enhances their flavor and helps to remove the tough outer skins. (Jalapeños and serranos need to be roasted only if you are going to freeze them.)

Before roasting, pierce the chilies a couple of times with a toothpick or sharp knife so that they will not explode when heated. To roast: Spear the chilies with a fork or skewer and hold them directly over the flame of a gas stove, or place them on a rack over an electric burner or on a foil-lined baking sheet approximately four inches from the heat source in a gas or electric broiler. No matter which method you choose, turn the chilies often to char the skins evenly. The chilies should be thoroughly blistered and somewhat blackened, but not burned through.

After charring, place the chilies in a paper bag and allow them to "sweat," or steam, for 10 to 20 minutes, which will further cook them and loosen the skins. If you plan to use the chilies immediately, remove them from the bag and peel off the skins with a sharp paring knife or rub under cold water (the skins should slip off easily). After peeling the chilies, remove the stems, unless you are making a dish that requires the chilies to hold their shape, such as Margaret Shakespeare's Zucchini-Stuffed Chilies (page 99). Seed and derib the chilies judiciously—remember that most of the hotness is in these parts of the chili, and they can create a startling experience for the uninitiated diner.

Roasted chilies freeze well. Do not peel them before freezing, as they will hold their shape better when thawed. Freeze a number of chilies in a plastic bag; you can remove one or two at a time when needed, since the chilies will not stick together when frozen. As the chilies thaw, you can peel the skins off easily. Seed and derib them if you want a milder flavor.

9

HANDLING CHILIES

The oils of chilies, concentrated in the seeds and ribs, contain a highly irritating substance, capsaicin, which, depending on the hotness of the chili, can cause a rash or even a burn. When handling all chilies—fresh, dried, canned, or powdered—take very great care to protect your skin. Work with whole chilies under cold running water (hot water can release irritating vapors). Wear thin rubber gloves or generously oil your hands. Do not touch your face, especially your eyes, until you have thoroughly washed your hands with soap and warm water. If you do touch your eyes, flush them with cold water immediately.

Pasilla: This long, thin, almost black chili is hotter than either the ancho or the mulato (the flesh is mild, but the seeds and veins are *very* hot). It is often sold at Mexican groceries. The ancho is an acceptable substitution.

Chipotle: A chipotle chili (usually a jalapeño) has been smoked with mesquite during the drying process. Chipotles are very hot. They are sometimes available canned. There is no substitute.

CANNED CHILIES

Canned chilies are marketed by a number of companies specializing in Mexican ingredients. The "mild, green" type, with no further identification on the label, is the most readily available and is an acceptable substitute for a large, fresh, green chili. Canned chilies come roasted and peeled, but may be diced, sliced, or whole. (See the recipes of Jane Butel and Rick Bayless on pages 18–25 and 54–63, respectively). Canned chilies labeled "jalapeño" or "serrano" are not roasted and peeled. All canned chilies should be rinsed, drained, and patted dry before use in recipes. Although canned chilies are not as hot as either fresh or dried, observe the usual precautions when handling them until you determine their potency.

DRIED CHILIES

Dried red chilies are vine-ripened green chilies, which turn from green to yellow to orange to red as they mature, then are picked and dried in the sun or in an oven. Dried chilies usually are sold in cellophane packets, or more strikingly, strung on long *ristras*, or strands. Good-quality dried chilies will be an even color, unbroken, and insect free. If you store them in a cool, dry place, dried chilies that are in perfect condition can last for several months. Tightly sealed in a plastic container and refrigerated or frozen, they will last indefinitely.

To prepare dried chilies for cooking, wipe off any surface dust. To soften them and intensify their flavor, roast them about one minute in a greaseless skillet, being careful not to scorch them. Set them in a colander under cold running water and, using the safety measures above, slit lengthwise, stem, seed, and derib. Then use them as the recipes indicate.

Dried chilies in this volume:

Ancho: The dried form of a poblano, this is the most common Mexican chili. It has a wrinkled, deep mahogany skin and varies from mild to medium-hot. It is widely available at Mexican groceries and at some supermarkets.

Mulato negro: Similar in appearance to the ancho but sweeter, this medium-hot chili dries almost black. Since it is not widely available, you may substitute the ancho.

Pequin: Very small (pea-sized) and extremely hot, this oval chili is often crushed before being added to a recipe. One quarter teaspoon of Cayenne pepper equals one pequin. Pequins are sold in some southwestern supermarkets, but are commonly found in Mexican groceries.

CHILI POWDERS

Some recipes in this volume call for "pure" chili powder, which contains chilies only, as distinct from powders that are a blend of chilies, cumin, oregano, onion, garlic, or salt. Other recipes simply call for "chili powder," indicating the blended type. If you want to make your own pure chili powder, grind prepared dried chilies to a powder in a blender or in a food processor. Several recipes call for "California (mild)" or "New Mexico (hot)" chili powders. These can be found in Mexican groceries or specialty stores. In any case, buy powder that is bright orange-red to dark red. A yellowish color indicates age or inferior quality. To ensure freshness, store chili powders in the refrigerator or freezer.

Grain Products

Many of the recipes in this volume call for the following ingredients made from corn and wheat:

MASA HARINA

This corn flour, made from dried corn kernels treated with lime, when mixed with water, produces the traditional dough for corn tortillas, tamales, and other recipes. Regular cornmeal, an entirely different product, is no sub-

Cooking at high temperatures can be dangerous, but not if you follow a few simple steps:

▶ Water added to hot fat will always cause spattering. If possible, pat foods dry with a cloth or paper towel before you add them to the hot oil in a skillet, Dutch oven, or wok.

▶ Lay the food in the pan gently, or the fat will certainly spatter.

▶ Be aware of your cooking environment. If you are boiling or steaming some foods while sautéing others, place the pots far enough apart so the water is unlikely to splash into the oil.

▶ Turn pot handles inward, toward the middle of the stove, so that you do not accidentally knock something over.

▶ Remember that alcohol—wine, brandy, or spirits—may occasionally catch fire when you add it to a very hot pan. If this happens, stand back for your own protection, and then quickly cover the pan with a lid. The fire will instantly subside, and the food will be just as good as ever.

▶ Keep pot holders and mitts close enough to be handy, but never hang them above the burners and do not lay them on the stove top.

---

stitute. Packaged in one- or five-pound bags, *masa harina* is on the shelf in many supermarkets and Mexican groceries. Store it tightly wrapped in a cool place for up to three months or refrigerate or freeze it indefinitely. Sue Huffman calls for *masa harina* in her Tamale Pie with Green Sauce (page 43).

TORTILLAS

Corn tortillas: These flat breads made from masa harina are eaten fresh, cut into sections and fried crisp for dipping or for a garnish, fried flat and layered with toppings *(tostadas),* stacked in casseroles, or used to wrap any number of fillings.

Blue-corn tortillas: Made from a special variety of indigo-blue corn grown in New Mexico, these are used in New Mexico-style dishes. Often hard to find, they are occasionally available at specialty food shops, but more likely available only through mail order (see page 103). Jane Butel calls for them in her Santa Fe-style enchiladas recipe (page 21). Substitute corn tortillas, if necessary.

Wheat tortillas: Used in northern Mexico cooking, these tortillas are made from wheat flour, lard or shortening, salt, and water. Because they are more delicate than corn, and do not stand up as well when fried or used in recipes containing a lot of liquid, you cannot use them interchangeably.

You will find fresh tortillas in the dairy section of many supermarkets or in Mexican groceries. Frozen tortillas are fine, but canned tortillas lack good taste and texture and are a poor substitute for either the fresh or the frozen. Refrigerate fresh tortillas, tightly wrapped in plastic bags and use them up as soon as possible. You can also freeze them, but allow an hour for thawing.

If you are going to fry them, first blot up moisture with a paper towel to prevent spattering. If they are stiff after refrigeration, make them pliable by steaming them. Or first dampen them, then fry or broil them for a few seconds on each side. There are many differences of opinion on the best way to fry a tortilla. Variations have mainly to do with the amount and temperature of the cooking oil. Recommendations range from a light surface greasing to three inches of oil at temperatures from medium-hot, to shimmering hot, to a specific 375 to 400 degrees on a deep-fat thermometer. A good rule is to heat the oil until a cube of bread sizzles and browns. Whatever your method, fry the tortilla until lightly brown on both sides, turning once with tongs, and drain on paper towels.

Beans

The beans used in Mexican cooking come in a variety of shapes and colors, and each type has its own special flavor and texture. In this volume, you will use primarily pinto, black, and kidney beans, served boiled in soups and stews, or mashed and then fried. Although Mexican cooks prefer dried beans, for time-saving reasons canned beans are suggested for the recipes in this volume. All varieties used here are available canned at any supermarket.

Pinto: These medium-size oval beans are pinkish-tan and speckled with brown spots (*pinto* means "painted" in Spanish). Their earthy flavor and mealy texture makes them ideal for use in chilis or for frying.

Black: Also known as turtle beans, black beans are small and flat with one white spot on their charcoal-colored skin. They are a good addition to soups because of their creamy texture.

Red kidney: These are large beans, shaped like a kidney, with a meaty flavor. They are often used as a substitute for pinto beans in chilies or in recipes calling for refried beans.

If you have time to spare, use dried beans. The following cooking tips apply to all varieties: Before cooking, wash beans in cold water and pick through them carefully to remove any tiny stones. Presoak them, in water to cover, eight hours or overnight. Discard the soaking water. Put the beans in a large pot with unsalted water to cover. Simmer them, covered, very slowly for 1½ to 3 hours, or until they are tender, stirring them occasionally with a wooden spoon. Add more boiling water as necessary during cooking to keep them from drying out. When the beans are cooked, add salt to taste. If you are not going to use the beans immediately, refrigerate them in a covered container after cooling. Do not discard the small amount of cooking liquid that may remain; it will be absorbed as you use the beans in these recipes.

11

Margaritas

Refreshing fruit-flavored drinks are perfect adjuncts to spicy Mexican food. At cocktail time, offer margaritas ("little daisies"), a slightly tart blend of tequila, crushed ice, lime juice, and Triple Sec, an orange-flavored liqueur. Classically, margaritas are served in chilled salt-rimmed cocktail glasses. Several sources claim credit for having created this cocktail, but whatever its origin, the margarita has been popular for many years.

Juice of 1 lime
Table salt
4 ice cubes, crushed
1½ ounce tequila
½ ounce Triple Sec or other orange-flavored liqueur

1. Fill a small bowl ½ inch full with salt.
2. Rub the rim of a chilled cocktail glass with a slice of lime and press the rim into the salt. Set aside.
3. Combine remaining ingredients in a cocktail shaker, cover, and shake vigorously. Strain the mixture into the prepared glass.

Yield: 1 cocktail

Fruits and Vegetables

The Mexican produce called for in this volume includes the following:

Avocado: The avocado is used for guacamole and in salads and soups. Select those that do not have soft brown spots. The fruit is ripe when it yields to gentle pressure. Ripen avocados at home by putting them into a paper bag and leaving them at room temperature for a few days. To speed ripening, place a tomato or banana in the bag with the avocado.

The best way to extract the rich flesh is to cut the avocado in half, remove its seed, and scoop out the flesh with a spoon. For neat slices, if you are using a variety with tough skin and tender flesh, do not peel the avocado first. Instead, with a sharp paring knife, make uniform slits through the skin from the stem end to the opposite end, cutting down to the seed. Peel the skin off each slice, then gently remove the slices with your finger and a knife blade.

Jícama: A crunchy tuber resembling a turnip, jícama tastes like a cross between an apple and a water chestnut. You can find whole or cut up jícama in well-stocked supermarkets and in Mexican groceries. Store whole jícama in the refrigerator in a plastic bag or sliced and immersed in water in a covered container. In her Menu 2, Vickie Simms uses jícama in a salad (see page 78).

Mango: The oval mango has a sweet, peach-pineapple flavor and juicy flesh that clings to a flat central pit. A ripe mango should be fragrant and soft to the touch. An immature mango is very bitter, so allow a few days for ripening at room temperature, if need be. Skin color is not a reliable criterion for ripeness, since ripe mangos, depending on the variety, range in color from green to deep red. Rely on your touch and smell. Most well-stocked supermarkets and greengrocers carry mangos. Refrigerate ripe mangos and use as quickly as possible.

Papaya: A native Mexican fruit that tastes something like a sweet muskmelon, the papaya has orangey flesh with a creamy texture and black peppercorn-like seeds in the center. Ripe papayas have yellow-orange skin and yield to gentle pressure. Select fruit that are smooth and unblemished. Handle papayas gently since they bruise easily. Ripen immature papayas at room temperature, and when they are soft, refrigerate them. Use within one week of ripening.

Pomegranate: A colorful autumn fruit the size of a large apple, a pomegranate has a tough rind which may vary in color from yellow to deep red. The tiny interior seeds and their aromatic crimson coating are edible. Pomegranates are sold in some supermarkets and most greengrocers. Select unblemished fruit with an unbroken rind. Store them in the refrigerator. To open a pomegranate, cut a small gash in the rind with a sharp paring knife and pry the fruit open with your thumbs. Break the pieces into smaller sections and, using your fingers, gently separate the seeds with the juicy red pulp surrounding them from the hard rind. You can freeze the seeds in a tightly sealed container for up to two weeks. Pomegranate juice is the basis for grenadine syrup, used by Elizabeth Schneider in her Pineapple-Tequila Cooler (page 34).

Tomatillos: Also called *tomates verdes*, tomatillos resemble small green tomatoes and are just as tart. They have a brown papery husk that you must remove before cooking. Buy fresh tomatillos in supermarkets or Mexican groceries, selecting those that range from green to yellow-green and are plump and firm. Store them *unwashed* in a paper bag in your refrigerator for up to three weeks. Canned tomatillos, sold in the Mexican food section of many supermarkets, are an acceptable substitute.

Other Ingredients

Cheeses: Chihuahua cheese, used in Margaret Shakespeare's Mexican Bean-Filled Rolls (see page 102), is spongy and slightly acidic. Mild Cheddar or Monterey Jack are good alternatives. *Queso fresco*, also known as Mexican white cheese, is a crumbly, slightly salty cheese resembling farmer cheese. Good substitutes are crumbled white Cheddar or mild feta. You can find both Mexican cheeses in a Mexican grocery.

Chorizo: Mexican chorizo sausage, unlike its smoked Spanish counterpart, is made with freshly ground pork seasoned with herbs, spices, and ground chilies. It is sold in links, either freshly made or canned in lard. Refrigerate well-wrapped chorizo for up to two weeks, or freeze it indefinitely. You can substitute mild Spanish chorizo. Vickie Simms calls for chorizo for her Omelets with Tomato-Chili Sauce (pages 74–75).

Coriander: Also known as cilantro or Chinese parsley, fresh coriander has a very pungent aroma and flavor. It resembles flat-leafed Italian parsley, but its leaves are a paler green. Select bunches without any signs of yellowing or decay and, if possible, with the roots still attached.

Refrigerate upright in a container of water covered with a plastic bag. Some supermarkets, as well as Mexican and Chinese groceries, stock coriander. Dried coriander is not a good substitute, nor is ground coriander seed, which has a very different flavor.

Mexican chocolate: Commercially packaged in round or square cakes, Mexican chocolate is sweetened and flavored with cinnamon, vanilla, and ground almonds. You can readily find it at Mexican groceries or specialty food shops. Store it in plastic wrap or foil in a cool place. To make your own, melt 3 ounces of dark sweet chocolate with ½ teaspoon of ground cinnamon and dashes of almond and vanilla extracts. Add this to the liquid portion of your recipe.

Pine nuts: The variety picked from native American trees in New Mexico and Arizona are called *piñones*, and are smaller than European or Oriental pine nuts. Regardless of origin, all pine nuts have a delicate sweet flavor. Health food stores and specialty food shops stock these nuts (often labeled as Indian nuts) shelled or unshelled. Because they are highly perishable, store shelled nuts in the refrigerator. They keep for up to three months. Unshelled nuts last for a year in the freezer.

Pumpkin and squash seeds: Also known as *pepitas*, these are available shelled or unshelled, salted or unsalted. For these recipes, use unsalted. Highly perishable, pepitas should be refrigerated. Elizabeth Schneider's recipe for Rock Cornish Hens in Fragrant Green Sauce (pages 28–29), is based on a traditional Mexican pumpkin-seed sauce for poultry. If you wish, combine leftover pepitas with nuts, raisins, or other dried fruit for a nutritious snack food.

COOKING TECHNIQUES

Sautéing

Sautéing is a form of quick frying with no cover on the pan. In French, *sauter* means "to jump," which is what vegetables or small pieces of food do when you shake the sauté pan. The purpose is to lightly brown the food and seal in the juices, sometimes before further cooking. This technique has three critical elements: the right pan, the proper temperature, and dry food.

The sauté pan: A proper sauté pan is 10 to 12 inches in diameter and has 2- to 3-inch straight sides that allow you to turn food pieces and still keep the fat from spattering. It has a heavy bottom that slides easily over a burner.

The best material (and the most expensive) for a sauté pan is tin-lined copper because it is a superior heat conductor. Heavy-gauge aluminum works well but will discolor acidic food like tomatoes. Therefore, you should not use aluminum if the food is to be cooked for more than twenty minutes after the initial browning. Another option is to select a heavy-duty sauté pan made of strong, heat-conductive aluminum alloys. This type of professional cookware is smooth and stick-resistant.

Select a sauté pan large enough to hold the pieces of food without crowding. The heat of the fat and the air spaces around and between the pieces facilitate browning.

Making Stock

Although canned chicken broth or stock is all right for emergencies, homemade chicken stock has a rich flavor that is hard to match. Moreover, the commercial broths—particularly the canned ones—are likely to be oversalted.

To make your own stock, save chicken parts as they accumulate and put them in a bag in the freezer; then have a rainy-day stock-making session, using the recipe below. The skin from a yellow onion will add color; the optional veal bone will add extra flavor and richness to the stock.

Basic Chicken Stock

3 pounds bony chicken parts, such as wings, back, and neck
1 veal knuckle (optional)
3 quarts cold water
1 yellow unpeeled onion, stuck with 2 cloves
2 stalks celery with leaves, cut in two
12 crushed peppercorns
2 carrots, scraped and cut into 2-inch lengths
4 sprigs parsley
1 bay leaf
1 tablespoon fresh thyme, or 1 teaspoon dried
Salt (optional)

1. Wash chicken parts and veal knuckle (if you are using it) and drain. Place in large soup kettle or stockpot (any big pot) with the remaining ingredients—except salt. Cover pot and bring to a boil over medium heat.

2. Lower heat and simmer stock, partly covered, 2 to 3 hours. Skim foam and scum from top of stock several times. Add salt to taste after stock has cooked 1 hour.

3. Strain stock through fine sieve placed over large bowl. Discard chicken pieces, vegetables, and seasonings. Let stock cool uncovered (this will speed cooling process). When completely cool, refrigerate. Fat will rise and congeal conveniently at top. You may skim it off and discard it or leave it as protective covering for stock.

Yield: About 10 cups.

Crowding results in steaming—a technique that lets the juices out rather than sealing them in. If your sauté pan is not large enough to prevent crowding, separate the food into two batches, or use two pans at once.

Be sure you buy a sauté pan with a tight-fitting cover. Many recipes call for sautéing first, then lowering the heat and cooking the food, covered, for an additional 10 to 20 minutes. Make certain the handle is long and is comfortable to hold.

Never immerse the hot pan in cold water because this will warp the metal. Allow the pan to cool slightly, then add water and let it sit until you are ready to wash it. Use a wooden spatula or tongs to keep food pieces moving in the pan as you shake it over the burner. If the food sticks, as it occasionally will, a metal spatula will loosen it best. Turn the pieces so that all surfaces come into contact with the hot fat and none of them sticks. Do not use a fork when sautéing meat; piercing the meat will toughen it.

Sangria

As a refreshing complement to Mexican cuisine, offer your guests a pitcher of *sangria*, an iced wine punch bolstered with brandy, orange-flavored liqueur, and orange juice. A classic thirst-quencher from Spain, *sangria* is now a very popular party drink in the United States. Use the basic recipe below, or experiment by using different fruit-flavored brandies, liqueurs, and fresh fruit.

1 bottle dry, full-bodied red wine
1½ ounces brandy
1 ounce orange-flavored liqueur, such as Cointreau or Triple Sec
¼ cup orange juice
¼ cup sugar, approximately
1 orange
1 lime
1 nectarine
Ice cubes
Club soda

1. In large pitcher, combine wine, brandy, liqueur, orange juice, and sugar to taste, and refrigerate.
2. Just before serving, wash fruit and pat dry. Slice orange and lime crosswise into ⅛-inch-thick rounds, and then cut orange rounds into quarters. Halve nectarine lengthwise and twist halves gently in opposite directions to separate. Remove pit and discard. Cut into thin wedges.
3. Remove pitcher from refrigerator, add ice cubes, fruit, and club soda to taste.
4. Pour into tall glasses and garnish each with a spoonful of the fresh fruit.

Yield: About 1 quart

The fat: A combination of half butter and half vegetable oil or peanut oil is perfect for most sautéing: it heats to high temperatures without burning and allows you to have a rich butter flavor at the same time. Always use unsalted butter for cooking, since it tastes better and does not add unwanted salt to your recipe.

Butter alone makes a superb tasting sauté, but butter, whether salted or unsalted, burns at a high temperature. If you prefer an all-butter flavor, clarify the butter before you begin. This means removing the milky residue, which is the part that scorches. To clarify butter, heat it in a small saucepan over medium heat and, using a cooking spoon, skim off the foam as it rises to the top and discard it. Keep skimming until no more foam appears. Pour off the remaining oil, making sure to leave the milky residue at the bottom of the pan. The oil is clarified butter; use this for sautés. Ideally, you should clarify butter as you need it. But it is a simple matter to make a large quantity of it and store it in your refrigerator; it will keep for two to three weeks. Some sautéing recipes in this book call for olive oil, which imparts a delicious and distinctive flavor and is less sensitive than butter to high heat. Nevertheless, even the finest olive oil has some residue of fruit pulp, which will scorch over high heat. Watch carefully when you sauté in olive oil; discard any scorched oil and start with fresh if necessary.

To sauté properly, heat the sauté fat until it is hot but not smoking. When you see small bubbles on top of the fat, it is almost hot enough to smoke. In that case, lower the heat and wait for the bubbling to stop. When using unclarified butter and oil together, add the butter to the hot oil. After the foam from the melting butter subsides, you are ready to sauté. If the temperature is just right, the food will sizzle when you put it in.

Poaching

You poach meat, fish, or chicken, even fruit, exactly as you would an egg, in very hot liquid in a shallow pan on top of the stove. You can use water, or better still, beef, chicken, or fish stock, or a combination of stock and white wine, or even cream. Bring the liquid to the simmering point and add the food. Be prepared to lower the heat if the liquid begins to boil. See Sue Huffman's Chicken Soup with Tortilla Strips (page 41), and Elizabeth Schneider's Chicken Mole Poblano (pages 94–95).

Blanching

Blanching, also called parboiling, is an invaluable technique. Immerse whole or cut vegetables for a few moments in boiling water, then "refresh" them—that is, plunge them into cold water to stop their cooking and set their colors. Blanching softens or tenderizes dense or crisp vegetables, often as a preliminary to further cooking by another method, such as stir frying.

Flambéing

Flambéing requires igniting an already-warm, but not close to boiling, liqueur in the pan with already-cooked hot food. Be sure to remove the pan from the heat first; then avert your face and ignite the liqueur with a lighted match. A quiet flame will burn for a few seconds. Allow about an ounce of liqueur per person. The taste remains, but the alcohol burns off—and you have enjoyed a moment of showmanship.

Broiling and Grilling

These are two relatively fast ways to cook meat, poultry and fish, giving the food a crisp exterior while leaving the inside juicy. For uniform cooking, flatten the pieces of food to an even thickness. Whether broiling or grilling, brush meat with melted fat, a sauce, or marinade before you cook. This adds flavor and keeps the food moist.

In broiling, the meat cooks directly under the heat source. To ensure proper cooking, move the broiling rack five or six inches from the heat source.

Roasting and Baking

Originally, *roasting* was the term for cooking meat on a revolving spit over an open fire, but now it means cooking meat or poultry in an oven by a dry-heat process. Roasting is especially suitable for thick cuts of meat and whole poultry. You should baste food several times with drippings or a flavorful basting sauce.

Equipment

Proper cooking equipment makes the work light and is a good cook's most prized possession. You can cook expertly without a store-bought steamer or even a food processor, but basic pans, knives, and a few other items are indispensable. Below are the things you need—and some attractive options—for preparing the menus in this volume.

Pots and pans

3 skillets (large, medium, small),
    with covers
7-inch omlet pan
3 saucepans with covers (1-, 2-, and
    4-quart capacities)
    Choose enameled cast-iron, plain
    cast-iron, aluminum-clad stainless
    steel, and heavy aluminum (but you
    need at least one saucepan that is not
    aluminum). Best—but very expen-
    sive—is tin-lined copper.
Roasting pan
Broiler pan
4 shallow baking pans (10 x 15-inch,
    9 x 13-inch, 9½ x 9½-inch, and
    8 x 8-inch)
Cookie sheet (11 x 17-inch)
12-cup muffin tin
9-inch pie plate
Platters

Knives

A carbon-steel knife takes a sharp
edge but tends to rust. You must
wash and dry it after each use; otherwise it can blacken foods and counter
tops. Good-quality stainless steel
knives, frequently honed, are less
trouble and will serve just as well in
the home kitchen. Never put a fine
knife in the dishwasher. Rinse it, dry
it, and put it away—but not loose in
a drawer. Knives will stay sharp and
last a long time if they have their own
storage rack.
Small paring knife (sharp-pointed
    end)
10-inch chef's knife
Bread knife
Sharpening steel

Other cooking tools

4 mixing bowls in graduated sizes,
    at least 1 nonaluminum
Colander, with a round base
    (stainless steel, aluminum, or
    enamel)
Strainers (preferably 2, in fine and
    coarse mesh)
Sieve, coarse and medium mesh

2-quart pitcher
Small jar with tight-fitting lid
2 sets of measuring cups and
    spoons in graduated sizes
    One for dry ingredients, another for
    shortenings and liquids.
Cooking spoon
Slotted spoon
Wooden spoons
Long-handled, 2-pronged fork
Metal spatula, or turner (for lifting
    hot foods from pans)
Slotted spatula
Rubber or vinyl spatula (for folding
    in hot or cold ingredients, off
    the heat)
Grater (metal, with several sizes of
    holes)
Wire whisk
Pair of metal tongs
Wooden cutting board
Potato masher
Garlic press
Vegetable peeler
Mortar and pestle
Soup ladle
Pastry brush for basting (a small,
    new paintbrush that is not
    nylon serves well)
Cake tester
Zester
Kitchen shears
Kitchen timer
Aluminum foil
Paper towels
Plastic wrap
Small brown paper bags
Wax paper
Thin rubber gloves

Electric appliances

Food processor or blender
    A blender will do most of the work
    required in this volume, but a food
    processor will do it more quickly and
    in larger volume. A food processor
    should be considered a necessity, not
    a luxury, for anyone who enjoys
    cooking.
Electric mixer

Optional cooking tools

Large cast-iron grilling pan
Wok
Salad spinner
Carving board
Carving knife
Oyster knife
Apple corer
Chinese wok spatulas
Cheese grater
Nut grinder
Citrus juicer
    Inexpensive glass kind from the
    dime store will do.
Apple corer
Melon baller
Pie server
Deep-fat thermometer
Roll of masking tape or white paper
    tape for labeling and dating

Pantry (for this volume)

A well-stocked, properly organized pantry is essential for preparing great meals in the shortest time possible. Whether your pantry consists of a small refrigerator and two or three shelves over the sink, or a large freezer, refrigerator, and entire room just off the kitchen, you must protect staples from heat and light.

In maintaining your pantry, follow these rules:

1. Store staples by kind and date. Canned goods, canisters, and spices need a separate shelf, or a separate spot on a shelf. Date all staples—shelved, refrigerated, or frozen—by writing the date directly on the package or on a bit of masking tape. Then put the oldest ones in front to be sure you use them first.

2. Store flour, sugar, and other dry ingredients in canisters or jars with tight lids. Glass and clear plastic allow you to see at a glance how much remains.

3. Keep a running grocery list so that you can note when a staple is half gone, and be sure to stock up.

ON THE SHELF:

Baking powder

Baking soda

Chilies, canned
jalapeños
mild green chilies
serranos

Dried fruits
raisins, dark and golden

Flour
all-purpose, bleached or unbleached
cornmeal
May be yellow or white and of various degrees of coarseness. The stone-ground variety, milled to retain the germ of the corn, generally has a superior flavor.

Garlic
Store in a cool, dry, well-ventilated place. Garlic powder and garlic salt are not adequate substitutes for fresh garlic.

Herbs and spices
The flavor of fresh herbs is much better than that of dried. Fresh herbs should be refrigerated and used as soon as possible. The following herbs are perfectly acceptable dried, but buy in small amounts, store airtight in dry area away from heat and light, and use as quickly as possible. In measuring herbs, remember that one part dried will equal three parts fresh. *Note:* Dried chives and parsley should not be on your shelf, since they have little or no flavor; frozen chives are acceptable. Buy whole spices rather than ground, as they keep their flavor much longer. Grind spices at home and store as directed for herbs.

basil

bay leaves

Cayenne pepper

chili peppers, whole and powdered

cinnamon, sticks and ground

cloves, whole and ground

coriander seeds

cumin

curry powder, preferably imported

dill

marjoram

mustard seeds and powdered

oregano

paprika

pepper
black peppercorns
These are unripe peppercorns dried in their husks. Grind with a pepper mill for each use.
white peppercorns
These are the same as the black variety, but are picked ripe and husked. Use them in pale sauces when black pepper specks would spoil the appearance.

red pepper flakes (also called crushed red pepper)

salt
Use coarse salt—commonly available as Kosher or sea—for its superior flavor, texture, and purity. Kosher salt and sea salt are less salty than table salt. Substitute in the following proportions: three quarters teaspoon table salt equals just under one teaspoon Kosher or sea salt.

sesame seeds

thyme

Honey

Hot pepper sauce

Nuts, whole, chopped or slivered
almonds
pecans
pine nuts (pignoli)
walnuts

Oils
corn, safflower, or vegetable
Because these neutral-tasting oils have high smoking points, they are good for high-heat sautéing.
olive oil
Sample French, Greek, Spanish, and Italian oils. Olive oil ranges in color from pale yellow to dark green and in taste from mild and delicate to rich and fruity. Different olive oils can be used for different purposes: for example, lighter ones for cooking, stronger ones for salads. The finest quality olive oil is labeled extra-virgin or virgin.
walnut oil
Rich and nutty tasting. It turns rancid easily, so keep it tightly closed in the refrigerator.

Onions
Store all dry-skinned onions in a cool, dry, well-ventilated place.
Bermuda onions
Large and mild, with a flattish shape, they are best baked whole or eaten raw, although they can be used in cooking. They are generally yellow but also may be red or white.
red or Italian onions
Zesty tasting and generally eaten raw. The perfect salad onion.
Spanish onions
Very large with a sweet flavor, they are best for stuffing and baking and are also eaten raw. Perfect for sandwiches.
yellow onions
All-purpose cooking onions, strong in taste.
white onions
Also called boiling onions, these small onions are almost always cooked and served whole.

Rice
long-grain white rice
Slender grains, much longer than they are wide, that become light and fluffy when cooked and are best for general use.

Stock, chicken
For maximum flavor and quality, your own stock is best (see recipes page 13), but canned stock, or broth, is adequate for most recipes and convenient to have on hand.

Sugar
dark brown sugar
granulated sugar

Tomatillos (tomates verdes)

Tomatoes

Italian plum tomatoes
Canned plum tomatoes (preferably imported) are an acceptable substitute for fresh.

tomato paste
Also for sauces. Spoon single tablespoons of unused canned paste onto wax paper and freeze them. Lift frozen paste off and store in plastic container. Sometimes available in tubes, which can be stored in the refrigerator after a small amount is used.

Vanilla extract

Vinegars

apple cider vinegar (also called cider vinegar)
Use for a mild, fruity flavor.

red and white wine vinegars

Wines and spirits

sherry, sweet and dry

red wine, dry

tequila

Kahlúa or other coffee-flavored liqueur

IN THE REFRIGERATOR:

Bread crumbs

You need never buy bread crumbs. To make fresh crumbs, use fresh or day-old bread and process in food processor or blender. For dried, toast bread 30 minutes in preheated 250-degree oven, turning occasionally to prevent slices from browning. Proceed as for fresh. Store bread crumbs in an airtight container: fresh crumbs in the refrigerator, and dried crumbs in a cool, dry place. Either type may also be frozen for several weeks if tightly wrapped in a plastic bag.

Butter

Many cooks prefer unsalted butter because of its finer flavor and because it does not burn as easily as salted.

Cheese

Cheddar cheese, sharp
A firm cheese, ranging in color from nearly white to yellow. Cheddar is a versatile cooking cheese.

Farmer cheese
An uncured cheese with a mild flavor, it is good substitute for Mexican *queso blanco* or *queso fresco*.

Monterey Jack cheese
A semisoft, whole-milk cheese, excellent for grating and melting.

Parmesan cheese
Avoid the pregrated packaged variety; it is very expensive and almost flavorless. Buy Parmesan by the quarter- or half-pound wedge and grate as needed: 4 ounces produces about one cup of grated cheese. Romano, far less costly, can be substituted, but its flavor is considerably sharper—or try mixing the two.

Coriander

Also called *cilantro* or Chinese parsley. Store coriander with the stems in a glass of water; cover leaves with a plastic bag.

Cream

half-and-half

heavy cream

sour cream

Eggs

Will keep 4 to 5 weeks in refrigerator. For best results, bring to room temperature before using.

Ginger, fresh

Found in the produce section. Ginger will stay fresh in the refrigerator for approximately 1 week, wrapped in plastic. To preserve it longer, place the whole ginger root in a small sherry-filled jar; it will last almost indefinitely, although not without changes in the ginger. Or, if you prefer, store it in the freezer, where it will last about 3 months. Newly purchased ginger need not be peeled.

Lemons

In addition to its many uses in cooking, a slice of lemon rubbed over cut apples and pears will keep them from discoloring. Do not substitute bottled juice or lemon extract.

Limes

Mayonnaise

Milk

Mint

Fresh mint will keep for a week if wrapped in a damp paper towel and enclosed in a plastic bag.

Mustards

The recipes in this book usually call for Dijon or coarse-ground mustard.

Parsley

The two most commonly available kinds of parsley are flat-leaved and curly; they can be used interchangeably when necessary. Flat-leaved parsley has a more distinctive flavor and is generally preferred in cooking. Curly parsley wilts less easily and is excellent for garnishing. Store parsley in a glass of water and cover loosely with a plastic bag. It will keep for a week in the refrigerator. Or wash and dry it, and refrigerate in a small plastic bag with a dry paper towel inside to absorb any moisture.

Scallions

Scallions have a mild onion flavor. Store wrapped in plastic.

Tortillas, corn and wheat flour

Jane Butel

L ike most smart cooks, Jane Butel knows that there are no substitutes for fresh, wholesome ingredients. Her insistence on using only "the freshest and purest" underlines her approach to Southwestern-style Mexican cooking. For these dishes to retain their authentic Mexican flavors, she suggests using only top-quality pure spices, seasonings, and other ingredients.

Although she has roamed the Southwest to discover traditional recipes and has worked with Pueblo Indian cooks in New Mexico, Jane Butel believes that Mexican meals should be interpretive. No cook need feel bound to follow her recipes and techniques exactly.

Just right for an informal brunch or light supper, Menu 1 features marinated scallops and open enchiladas with fried eggs. Sweet peppers and cumin rice in Menu 2 accompany chicken tacos, a popular dish in Mexico as well as in the United States. For dessert, serve rich chocolate sundaes with Kahlúa, a Mexican coffee-flavored liqueur, which is spooned into the bottom of each bowl.

Texans are credited with inventing *chili con carne*—a stew-like dish of cubed beef simmered in a spicy sauce— but there are probably as many versions of chili as there are cooks. Jane Butel's chili recipe in Menu 3 is a perfect example of her individualistic approach to cooking. You can personalize her chili by varying the suggested garnishes to suit your taste. New Mexican refried beans and a substantial salad complete this meal.

Fresh flowers and colorful pottery dishes set the tone for this cheery brunch. Top each of the easily assembled open enchiladas with a fried egg and garnish the plates with lettuce and a halved cherry tomato. The marinated scallops, with their dressing of onions and peppers, sit on a bed of lettuce.

Marinated Scallops
Sante Fe-Style Open Enchiladas with Fried Eggs

For an impressive meal that looks complicated but isn't, prepare marinated scallops as a first course or as a salad to go with the enchiladas.

The Santa Fe-style open enchiladas consist of lightly fried tortillas layered with grated cheese, chopped onion, and spicy red chili sauce and topped with a fried egg. Jane Butel prefers to use blue-corn tortillas but regular corn tortillas work just as well. (For information about tortillas, see page 11.)

WHAT TO DRINK

Serve cold beer or ale, a well-chilled white wine, such as a crisp, acidic Verdicchio or Muscadet, or even fresh lemonade with this menu.

SHOPPING LIST AND STAPLES

1 pound bay scallops
Small head Romaine lettuce
Small head leaf lettuce
4 cherry tomatoes
Large green bell pepper
Large Spanish onion
Medium-size purple onion
4 cloves garlic
1 fresh jalapeño or 4-ounce can
2 limes
4 eggs
4 tablespoons unsalted butter
¼ pound Muenster cheese
¼ pound Cheddar cheese
1 quart beef stock, preferably homemade, or canned
¼ cup olive oil
½ cup vegetable oil
2 tablespoons wine vinegar, preferably white
1 dozen 6-inch corn tortillas, preferably blue-corn
¼ cup flour
½ cup California (mild), New Mexican (hot), or other pure chili powder
Ground oregano, preferably Mexican
Ground cumin
Crushed red pepper flakes (optional)
Salt and freshly ground pepper

UTENSILS

Large skillet
Small skillet.

2 medium-size saucepans, one heavy-gauge
Platter
4 ovenproof dinner plates
Medium-size bowl
Salad spinner (optional)
Measuring cups and spoons
Chef's knife
Paring knife
Wooden spoon
Metal spatula
Rubber spatula
Grater
Whisk
Tongs

START-TO-FINISH STEPS

1. Peel and mince garlic for scallops and chili sauce.
2. Follow scallops recipe steps 1 through 5.
3. For scallops and enchiladas recipes, rinse lettuce and dry in salad spinner or pat dry with paper towels. Reserve 8 leaves of leaf lettuce for scallops. Tear remaining lettuce into 2-inch square pieces. Wrap all in paper towels and refrigerate.
4. Follow chili sauce recipe steps 1 through 3.
5. Follow enchiladas recipe steps 1 through 5, and sauce recipe step 4.
6. Follow scallops recipe step 6 and serve.
7. Follow enchiladas recipe steps 6 through 10 and serve.

RECIPES

Marinated Scallops

2 limes
1 fresh jalapeño, washed and patted dry, or 1 canned, rinsed and drained
Medium-size purple onion
Large green bell pepper
¼ cup olive oil
1 tablespoon jalapeño juice, if using canned jalapeño
2 cloves garlic, peeled and minced
Pinch of ground oregano, preferably Mexican
Pinch of ground cumin
1 pound bay scallops
2 tablespoons wine vinegar, preferably white
Salt and freshly ground pepper
8 leaves leaf lettuce
Crushed red pepper flakes (optional)

1. Squeeze enough lime to measure 3 tablespoons juice. Prepare jalapeño (see pages 9, 10) and cut into ⅛-inch-thick slices. Peel onion and slice thinly. Rinse green pepper and pat dry. Halve, core, and seed pepper. Cut pepper into ⅛-inch julienne.

2. In large skillet, combine lime juice, 2 tablespoons olive oil, jalapeño slices to taste, jalapeño juice, if using, garlic, oregano, and cumin and bring to a boil over medium heat.

3. Add scallops, stirring continuously. Reduce heat and simmer 3 to 5 minutes, or until scallops have whitened and become firm. Remove skillet from heat and transfer mixture to medium-size bowl.

4. Return skillet to medium heat and add remaining olive oil. Add onion and green pepper, and sauté, stirring frequently, about 5 minutes, or just until crisp-tender.

5. Remove skillet from heat, add vinegar and salt and pepper to taste, and stir to blend. Set mixture aside, stirring occasionally.

6. Line 4 plates with lettuce and top with scallops. Stir sauce and pour over scallops. Sprinkle with red pepper flakes if desired.

Santa Fe-Style Open Enchiladas with Fried Eggs

¼ pound Muenster cheese
¼ pound Cheddar cheese
Large Spanish onion
½ cup vegetable oil, approximately
1 dozen 6-inch corn tortillas, preferably blue-corn
Red Chili Sauce (see following recipe)
4 eggs
4 cherry tomatoes
2 cups Romaine and leaf lettuce, torn into 2-inch pieces

1. Shred enough Muenster and Cheddar cheese to measure 1 cup each. Peel onion and chop finely. Halve tomatoes.

2. Preheat oven to 250 degrees.

3. In small skillet, heat oil over medium-high heat.

4. Line platter with paper towels and place 4 heatproof dinner plates in oven.

5. When oil is almost smoking, lightly fry tortillas, one at a time, about 10 seconds, or just until soft. Do not let tortillas become crisp. As they are done, transfer tortillas to paper-towel-lined platter, layering tortillas between towels. When all are done, if not preparing enchiladas immediately, cover platter loosely with foil and place in oven. Reserve oil in skillet.

6. Remove dinner plates and tortillas from oven and raise oven temperature to 350 degrees.

7. To assemble enchiladas, place a dollop of sauce on each plate and top with a tortilla. Top each tortilla with sauce, a spoonful or two of mixed cheeses, and a sprinkling of onion. Cover with another tortilla and then repeat with remaining tortillas and toppings. Place plates in oven until cheese has melted, about 5 minutes.

8. Meanwhile, wash, pat dry, and halve cherry tomatoes.

9. Using skillet in which tortillas were cooked, fry eggs 1 at a time. Top each enchilada with a fried egg.

10. Garnish each plate with lettuce and 2 cherry tomato halves. Serve additional sauce separately, if desired.

Red Chili Sauce

1 quart beef stock
4 tablespoons unsalted butter
¼ cup flour
½ cup pure chili powder
2 cloves garlic, peeled and minced
Pinch of ground cumin
Pinch of ground oregano, preferably Mexican
Salt

1. In medium-size saucepan, bring beef stock to a boil over medium heat.

2. In another medium-size heavy-gauge saucepan, melt butter over medium heat. When butter foams, add flour and cook, stirring, until mixture turns a light gold, about 3 minutes. Remove pan from heat.

3. Stir in chili powder and gradually add beef stock, whisking until smooth. Add garlic, cumin, and oregano.

4. Stirring constantly, bring sauce to a simmer over medium-high heat. Adjust heat to maintain a gentle simmer and cook ten minutes. Add salt to taste and set aside.

ADDED TOUCH

This New Mexico-style dish, based on an old Indian recipe, is best in summer when all the vegetables are at the peak of their flavor.

Squash with Tomatoes and Corn

3 to 4 fresh green chilies, roasted, peeled, and seeded, or 4-ounce can, rinsed, drained, and patted dry
3 small zucchini (about 1 pound total weight)
2 small yellow crookneck summer squash (about ¾ pound total weight)
2 large ripe tomatoes (about 1 pound total weight), or 16-ounce can, drained
2 ears fresh corn, or 10-ounce package frozen, thawed
Salt
2 tablespoons unsalted butter
1 teaspoon minced fresh coriander, approximately

1. Prepare chilies (see pages 9, 10).

2. Wash squash, pat dry, and slice thinly.

3. Core, halve, and seed fresh tomatoes, if using, and cut each half into quarters. If using canned tomatoes, drain. Hull fresh corn or measure 1 cup frozen. Chop chilies.

4. Heat ¼-inch water in medium-size saucepan over medium-high heat. Add squash and steam until barely tender, 3 to 4 minutes.

5. Add tomatoes, corn and chilies to squash, stir to combine, and cook until crisp tender, about 3 to 5 minutes. Add salt to taste.

6. Wash coriander and pat dry. Mince enough to measure 1 teaspoon.

7. Top vegetables with butter and coriander to taste. Toss to combine, cover, and keep warm until ready to serve.

Chicken Tacos
Sweet Peppers and Cumin Rice
New Mexican Chocolate Sundaes

Three chicken tacos and a portion of sweet peppers and cumin rice make a filling lunch or dinner.

Taco shells are sold ready-made in supermarkets but are easy to make at home: Pour half an inch of vegetable oil into a skillet. Heat the oil until a cube of fresh bread sizzles and floats to the surface of the oil. Lightly fry each tortilla on one side and, while it is still pliable, turn the tortilla over and fold it in half. Fry each folded tortilla, turning it until it is crisp on both sides.

WHAT TO DRINK

A light pilsner beer or a spicy wine, such as a Gewürztraminer, would interact very nicely with these dishes.

SHOPPING LIST AND STAPLES

1 pound boned and skinned chicken breasts
Medium-size tomato
Small head Iceberg lettuce
Medium-size red bell pepper
Medium-size green bell pepper
3 bunches scallions
Medium-size Spanish onion
3 cloves garlic
3 fresh jalapeños, or 4-ounce can
½ pint heavy cream

1 quart good-quality vanilla ice cream
2 tablespoons unsalted butter
¼ pound Monterey Jack cheese
¼ pound Cheddar cheese
2 cups chicken stock, preferably homemade (see page 13), or canned
4½-ounce package taco shells
1½ cups long grain rice
4 ounces sweet chocolate
3-ounce can pecan halves
1½ teaspoons cumin
½ teaspoon ground oregano, preferably Mexican
1 teaspoon cinnamon
½ teaspoon ground cloves
Salt and freshly ground pepper
¼ cup Kahlúa, preferably, or other coffee liqueur

UTENSILS

2 medium-size heavy-gauge saucepans with covers
2 small heavy-gauge saucepans
11 × 17-inch cookie sheet
1 large bowl
2 medium-size bowls
2 small bowls
Measuring cups and spoons
Chef's knife
Paring knife
Slotted spoon
Wooden spoon
Grater

START-TO-FINISH STEPS

1. Follow tacos recipe step 1.
2. Follow rice recipe steps 1 through 5.
3. Follow sundaes recipe step 1.
4. Follow tacos recipe steps 2 through 6.
5. Follow sundaes recipe steps 2 and 3.
6. Follow rice recipe step 6.
7. Follow tacos recipe steps 7 and 8, and serve with rice.
8. Follow sundaes recipe step 4 and serve.

RECIPES

Chicken Tacos

1 pound boned and skinned chicken breasts
2 cups chicken stock
12 taco shells
Medium-size Spanish onion, peeled and minced
1 clove garlic, peeled and minced
Medium-size tomato, diced
2 cups shredded Iceberg lettuce
1 cup shredded Monterey Jack and Cheddar cheese combined
3 jalapeños, finely minced

1. Preheat oven to 250 degrees.
2. Combine chicken and stock in medium-size saucepan

and bring to a simmer over medium-high heat. Cover and simmer 15 to 20 minutes, or until chicken is tender.
3. Transfer chicken and stock to a medium-size bowl and set bowl, uncovered, in larger bowl filled with cold water.
4. Arrange taco shells on cookie sheet and place in oven with 4 dinner plates.
5. Combine onion, garlic, and tomato in small bowl.
6. Drain chicken, reserving stock for rice recipe. Cut chicken into ⅛-inch julienne strips. Place strips in another bowl, barely moisten with stock, cover, and set aside.
7. Remove taco shells and plates from oven and raise oven temperature to 400 degrees. Divide chicken, lettuce, and tomato mixture among taco shells and top with cheese.
8. Return tacos to oven for 1 minute, or just until cheese melts. Transfer to dinner plates and top with jalapeños.

Sweet Peppers and Cumin Rice

3 bunches scallions
Medium-size red bell pepper
Medium-size green bell pepper
1½ cups chicken stock (reserved from taco recipe)
2 tablespoons unsalted butter
2 cloves garlic, peeled and minced
1½ teaspoons cumin
½ teaspoon ground oregano, preferably Mexican
1½ cups long grain rice

1. Wash scallions, pat dry, and chop enough of white portion to measure 1½ cups. Reserve greens for other use. Halve, core, seed, and dice bell peppers.
2. In small saucepan, bring chicken stock to a boil over medium heat.
3. In large heavy-gauge saucepan, melt butter over medium heat. Add scallions and peppers, and cook, stirring frequently, until soft.
4. Stir in garlic, cumin, oregano, and rice.
5. Stir in stock. Lower heat, cover, and simmer 15 minutes without uncovering.
6. Taste rice, adjust seasoning, and return to heat, if necessary. Keep covered until ready to serve.

New Mexican Chocolate Sundaes

½ cup Kahlúa, preferably, or other coffee liqueur
1 quart good-quality vanilla ice cream
4 ounces sweet chocolate
1 cup heavy cream
1 teaspoon cinnamon
½ teaspoon ground cloves
12 pecan halves

1. Place 1 tablespoon Kahlúa in each dessert dish, top with scoops of ice cream, and place in freezer.
2. Break chocolate into pieces and place in small heavy-gauge pan over medium-low heat.
3. As chocolate melts, gradually add cream, stirring to combine each addition. Add cinnamon and cloves, and stir until blended. Cover pan and remove from heat.
4. Spoon sauce over ice cream and garnish with pecans.

Chili with No Beans
New Mexican Refried Beans
Western Salad with Avocado Dressing

Bowls of piping hot chili are ideal for a cold-weather meal. This quick version calls for sirloin steak, but you can use chuck, a less tender but more flavorful cut of beef, and simmer the cubes in the spicy liquid for two hours or longer. Garnish the chili with any, or all, of these toppings: chopped onions, chopped jalapeños, crushed pequín chilies, sour cream, and lime wedges.

The substantial Western salad is served with a creamy avocado-based dressing; the acid in the lime juice helps to retain the avocado's bright color.

WHAT TO DRINK

Start with margaritas (see page 12) and continue with sangria or switch to beer.

SHOPPING LIST AND STAPLES

3 pounds top sirloin, cut into ½-inch cubes
¼ pound thick-cut homestyle bacon
Large head Romaine lettuce
Medium-size bunch watercress
1 pint cherry tomatoes
Medium-size avocado
Medium-size bunch scallions
Large yellow onion
5 large cloves garlic
1 fresh jalapeño, or 4-ounce can
1 lime
16-ounce can pinto beans
3½-ounce can pitted black olives
2 tablespoons unsalted butter
¼ pound Monterey Jack cheese
¼ pound Cheddar cheese
¼ cup olive oil, approximately
¼ cup red or white wine vinegar, approximately
6-ounce bag tostaditas (tortilla chips)
1 ounce pure California (mild) chili powder
1 ounce pure New Mexican (hot) chili powder
2 teaspoons ground cumin
2 teaspoons oregano, preferably Mexican
Salt and freshly ground pepper
Two 12-ounce bottles beer or 2 cups red wine

Casual serving bowls are ideal for the beef chili, refried beans, and the Western salad—a meal best served buffet style. For an authentic touch, garnish the salad with tostaditas. Pass warmed French bread, if you wish.

UTENSILS

Large heavy-gauge skillet
Large heavy-gauge saucepan

Small saucepan
Salad bowl
Large bowl
Medium-size bowl
Small bowl
Platter
Plate
Measuring cups and spoons
Chef's knife
Paring knife
Slotted spoon
Wooden spoon
Potato masher (optional)
Grater

START-TO-FINISH STEPS

1. For chili recipe and beans recipe, peel and mince garlic. Grate cheeses and combine in small bowl.
2. Follow salad recipe steps 1 through 3.
3. Follow chili recipe steps 1 through 5.
4. While beef is cooking, follow beans recipe steps 1 through 4.
5. Follow chili recipe steps 6 and 7, beans recipe step 5, salad recipe steps 4 and 5, and serve.

RECIPES

Chili with No Beans

Large yellow onion
2 tablespoons unsalted butter
3 pounds top sirloin, cut into ½-inch cubes
1½ tablespoons minced garlic
¼ cup pure California (mild) chili powder
¼ cup pure New Mexican (hot) chili powder
2 teaspoons ground cumin
2 teaspoons oregano, preferably Mexican, crushed
1½ teaspoons salt
2 cups beer or red wine
1 cup grated Monterey Jack and Cheddar cheese combined

1. Peel and chop onion.
2. In large heavy-gauge saucepan, melt butter over medium heat. Add onions and cook, stirring frequently, about 5 minutes, or until transparent.
3. While onions are cooking, combine meat with garlic, chili powder, cumin, oregano, and salt in large bowl.
4. Bring 2 cups beer or red wine and 2 cups water to a boil in small saucepan over medium-high heat.
5. Add one quarter of meat to saucepan with onions, raise heat to medium-high, and cook, stirring, about 2 to 3 minutes, until meat has browned lightly and is encrusted with spices. Transfer to platter and repeat with remaining meat.
6. Return all meat to saucepan, add hot liquid, and stir to combine. Adjust heat to a simmer and cook, uncovered, 10 to 15 minutes, or until meat is tender.

7. If cooking liquid has not reduced to form a thick sauce, remove meat from pan with slotted spoon and, stirring constantly, reduce sauce over medium-high heat. Return meat to saucepan and stir. Turn chili into large serving bowl and top with grated cheese.

New Mexican Refried Beans

3 strips thick-cut homestyle bacon
Medium-size bunch scallions
2 tablespoons minced garlic
2 cups pinto beans, with liquid
Salt and freshly ground pepper
½ cup grated Monterey Jack and Cheddar cheese combined

1. Cut bacon into ½-inch squares. Wash scallions, pat dry, and chop enough to measure ¼ cup plus 2 tablespoons. Line plate with paper towels.
2. Cook bacon in large heavy-gauge skillet over medium heat, stirring, until it is crisp, about 5 minutes. With slotted spoon, transfer bacon to plate.
3. Add ¼ cup scallions and garlic to skillet and sauté over medium heat until they start to turn golden.
4. Add beans with their liquid and stir to combine. Toss and mash beans with potato masher or back of spoon until all liquid has been absorbed and beans are of uniform consistency. Add bacon and salt and pepper to taste.
5. Transfer beans to medium-size serving bowl and top with grated cheese and remaining scallions.

Western Salad with Avocado Dressing

Large head Romaine lettuce
Medium-size bunch watercress
16 cherry tomatoes
½ cup pitted black olives
Medium-size avocado
1 lime
½ jalapeño, approximately, finely minced
Salt and freshly ground pepper
¼ cup olive oil
¼ cup red or white wine vinegar
Tostaditas (tortilla chips), optional

1. Wash lettuce, watercress, and tomatoes, and pat dry. Tear lettuce and watercress into bite-size pieces. Halve olives crosswise. Combine lettuce, watercress, tomatoes, and olives in salad bowl. Cover and refrigerate.
2. Squeeze enough lime to measure ½ teaspoon juice. Prepare jalapeño (see pages 9, 10).
3. Halve avocado lengthwise, remove pit, and discard. Scoop flesh into medium-size bowl and mash roughly with fork. Add lime juice and jalapeño, and stir to combine. Adjust seasoning, adding salt, pepper, lime juice, and jalapeño as desired, cover, and refrigerate.
4. Pour oil over salad and toss until well coated. Add vinegar, toss again, and add salt and pepper to taste.
5. Spoon avocado mixture into center of salad and serve surrounded by tostaditas, if desired.

Elizabeth Schneider

When she was a novice cook, Elizabeth Schneider insisted on only authentic ingredients and recipes. However, with time and experience, she discovered that going by the book did not matter as much as making simple, high-quality meals with the freshest ingredients. So, too, she has found that American cooks tend to be unconventional, mixing and matching cuisines and adapting ingredients to suit their own tastes. In this spirit, Elizabeth Schneider enjoys experimenting with Mexican foods, particularly the dishes of New Mexico.

Menu 1, a festive year-round dinner, offers more traditional Mexican fare, Rock Cornish game hens in a green sauce resembling both *mole verde* (herbal green sauce) and *pollo en pipián* (chicken in pumpkin seed sauce), while Menus 2 and 3 are both vegetarian hybrids in the New Mexico style. The main course of Menu 2, suitable for lunch or a family supper, is green chili and cheese enchiladas filled with a combination of farmer cheese and sour cream. In Menu 3, the main course is a corn pudding—containing fresh corn kernels, cornmeal, chilies, and bits of cheese—a combination of southwestern tamale pie, southern spoonbread, and northeastern corn custard.

Casual pottery underlines the simple elegance of game hens coated with a thick green sauce, sprinkled with pumpkin seeds, and served with rice tossed with diced pimientos—a meal for family or company. A two-toned salad of lime green kiwi and red grapefruit slices, arranged on watercress, accompanies the main course.

Rock Cornish Hens in Fragrant Green Sauce
Rice with Cumin and Pimiento
Grapefruit, Kiwi, and Watercress Salad

The Rock Cornish game hen is a delicate foil for spicy sauces, such as "fragrant green." Weighing about one and one half pounds, it is ideal for two servings. For this recipe, the hens are poached in stock, a method that Mexican cooks often use. To prepare the sauce, which contains tomatillos and chilies, you can use either a food processor or a blender. For information about these ingredients, see pages 9, 10, and 12.

The salad calls for kiwis—fuzzy, brown-skinned oval fruit with lime-green flesh and melon-like texture. A perfectly ripe kiwi yields slightly to the touch.

WHAT TO DRINK

A French Pouilly Fumé or Sancerre or a California Sauvignon Blanc would go well here as would a pale ale.

SHOPPING LIST AND STAPLES

2 large Rock Cornish hens, quartered (about 3 pounds total weight)
Large bunch watercress
Small bunch scallions
Large bunch coriander
Medium-size bunch mint
Large clove garlic
3 large, medium-hot, fresh green chilies, or 4-ounce can
2 medium-size ruby red or pink grapefruit (about 2 pounds total weight)
3 kiwis
1 lemon
1⅔ cups chicken stock, preferably homemade (see page 13), or canned
13-ounce can tomatillos, or 14 to 18 fresh tomates verdes
4-ounce jar whole pimiento
2 tablespoons olive oil
2 tablespoons vegetable oil, plus 1 tablespoon (if not using walnut oil)
1 tablespoon walnut oil (optional)
1 tablespoon cider vinegar
2 teaspoons honey
1½ cups long-grain white rice
4-ounce bag pepitas (hulled pumpkin or squash seeds)
2 slices white bread
1½ teaspoons paprika
1 teaspoon ground cumin
Ground cinnamon
Salt and freshly ground pepper

UTENSILS

Food processor or blender
Large skillet with cover
Small skillet
Large, heavy-gauge saucepan with cover
Medium-size saucepan
Platter
Small bowl
Salad spinner (optional)
Measuring cups and spoons
Chef's knife
Paring knife
Wooden spoon
Long, double-pronged fork
Rubber spatula
Juicer (optional)
Tongs
Vegetable peeler

START-TO-FINISH STEPS

1. Wash coriander and mint for Cornish hens recipe and watercress for salad. Dry in salad spinner or pat dry with paper towels. Coarsely chop coriander and mint, and set aside. Wrap watercress in paper towels and refrigerate until needed. Juice lemon for salad dressing; reserve.
2. Follow rice recipe steps 1 through 5.
3. Follow Cornish hens recipe steps 1 through 8.
4. Follow salad recipe steps 1 through 4.
5. Follow rice recipe step 6, Cornish hens recipe step 9, and salad recipe step 5.

RECIPES

Rock Cornish Hens in Fragrant Green Sauce

1⅔ cups chicken stock
6 tablespoons pepitas (hulled pumpkin or squash seeds), plus 2 tablespoons for garnish
2 large Rock Cornish hens, quartered (about 3 pounds total weight)
13-ounce can tomatillos, or 14 to 18 fresh tomates verdes
3 large, medium-hot, green chilies, roasted, peeled, and seeded, or 3 canned chilies, rinsed, drained, and patted dry
2 slices white bread
4 scallions

1 cup coarsely chopped fresh coriander, packed
1 cup coarsely chopped fresh mint, packed

1. In large skillet, bring stock to a simmer over medium heat.
2. While stock is heating, toast pepitas in small skillet over medium heat, stirring frequently, about 2 to 3 minutes, or until they puff up. (Some pepitas "explode.") Set aside.
3. Add hens to stock, reduce heat to low, cover and simmer, turning once, 16 minutes, or until firm and juices run clear when hens are pierced with fork.
4. Meanwhile, if using canned tomatillos, rinse, drain, and pat dry or, if using tomatoes verdes, remove rough outer layer, rinse, and pat dry. In medium-size saucepan, simmer tomatillos in water to cover, over low heat 8 to 10 minutes, or until almost soft.
5. Prepare chilies (see pages 9, 10). Cut white bread into cubes. Trim scallions, cut off white portion, and reserve for another use. Wash green portion, pat dry with paper towels, and coarsely chop.
6. In food processor fitted with metal blade or in blender, chop cubed bread. Add 6 tablespoons toasted pepitas and process mixture until finely chopped. Drain tomatillos, add to bread crumb-pepita mixture, and chop. In succession, add chilies, scallions, coriander, and mint, chopping after each addition.
7. Remove hens from stock and set aside. For sauce, add stock to mixture in processor or blender and purée.
8. Return hens to skillet and combine with sauce. Simmer 10 minutes, turning once.
9. Arrange 2 hen quarters on each of 4 plates, spooning some sauce over each quarter. Garnish with remaining pepitas and serve remaining sauce separately.

Rice with Cumin and Pimiento

Large clove garlic
4-ounce jar whole pimiento
1½ cups long-grain white rice
2 tablespoons olive oil
1½ teaspoons paprika
1 teaspoon ground cumin
1 teaspoon salt

1. Peel and mince garlic. Drain pimiento and cut into ½-inch dice.
2. In heavy-gauge saucepan, heat oil over medium-high heat. Add rice and garlic, and cook 2 to 3 minutes, or until lightly browned.
3. Add paprika and cumin and cook, stirring, 1 minute.
4. Add salt and 2½ cups water and, stirring, bring to a rolling boil, over high heat. Add pimiento.
5. Reduce heat to low, cover, and cook 20 minutes. Without uncovering, remove pan from heat and let stand until serving time (up to 40 minutes, or until water is absorbed).
6. Fluff rice with fork and divide among 4 plates.

Grapefruit, Kiwi, and Watercress Salad

2 medium-size ruby red or pink grapefruit (about
    2 pounds total weight)
3 kiwis
2 tablespoons lemon juice
1 tablespoon cider vinegar
¼ teaspoon salt
1 tablespoon walnut oil, preferably, or vegetable oil
2 tablespoons vegetable oil
2 teaspoons honey
Large bunch watercress
Ground cinnamon
Freshly ground pepper

1. Peel grapefruit and remove pith. Cut each in half lengthwise and then slice crosswise into ½-inch-thick semicircles. Set aside.
2. Peel kiwi fruit and slice into ⅛- to ¼-inch-thick rounds. Set aside.
3. Prepare dressing: In small bowl, combine lemon juice, vinegar, and salt. Drain any accumulated grapefruit juice into dressing. Stir with fork until salt dissolves. Add walnut oil, vegetable oil, and honey, and beat until blended. Set aside.
4. Arrange watercress around edge of decorative platter. Overlap grapefruit slices in ring within watercress and arrange kiwi slices in center.
5. Just before serving, beat dressing to recombine and pour over salad. Sprinkle with cinnamon and pepper to taste.

Kiwi fruit

Avocado Soup
Green Chili and Cheese Enchiladas
Carrot, Apple, and Walnut Salad

In New Mexico, green chili and cheese enchiladas often are made with fragile blue-corn tortillas (see page 11 for information), which break easily when rolled. These are difficult to find in some areas of the country, so this recipe calls for standard corn tortillas, preferably fresh, or, if unavailable, frozen ones.

If you can find blue tortillas, bake them flat: Spread one third of the sauce in the bottoms of two 13 x 9 x 2-inch baking dishes. Add another third of the sauce to the farmer-cheese filling. Place two blue-corn tortillas, edges

Vivid textile patterns and informal tableware set off this New Mexico-style meal of carrot, apple, and walnut salad, smooth and rich avocado soup, and enchiladas garnished with radishes and Romaine lettuce.

not touching, on the sauce in each baking dish. Using half of the cheese filling, spread a layer on each tortilla. Top with another layer of tortillas and the rest of the cheese mixture, spreading it to the edges of the tortillas. Add a final layer of tortillas and spread the remaining green chili sauce on top. Sprinkle the grated cheese over all, and bake in a 350-degree oven about 15 minutes, or until the cheese melts and the sauce bubbles.

WHAT TO DRINK

If you want to depart from beer, serve a dry sparkling wine. Your options are many, ranging from nonvintage Champagne through Spanish, Italian, California, and New York sparkling wines.

SHOPPING LIST AND STAPLES

2 medium-size avocados
1 pound carrots
Small head Romaine lettuce (about ¾ pound)
Small bunch radishes
6 large, medium-hot, fresh green chilies,
    or two 4-ounce cans
Small bunch coriander
Small bunch scallions
Small clove garlic
2 medium-size crisp red apples, such as Winesap or
    Cortland (about ¾ pound total weight)
1 to 2 limes
2 cups buttermilk
½ pint sour cream
½ pound farmer cheese
¼ pound sharp Cheddar cheese
5 tablespoons corn oil
¼ cup cider vinegar
2 teaspoons sugar
12 fresh corn tortillas, or 1 package frozen
3-ounce can walnut pieces
1 teaspoon ground cumin
1 teaspoon freshly ground coriander seeds, or
    1 to 2 teaspoons packaged ground coriander

Salt
Freshly ground white pepper

UTENSILS

Food processor or blender
Small saucepan
13 x 9 x 2-inch baking/serving dish
Baking sheet or tray
Large bowl
3 small bowls
Salad spinner (optional)
Measuring cups and spoons
Chef's knife
Paring knife
Metal spoon
Metal spatula
Grater (if not using food processor)
Juicer (optional)
Pastry brush
Vegetable peeler

START-TO-FINISH STEPS

One hour ahead: Refrigerate avocados for soup recipe. If using frozen tortillas for enchiladas recipe, set out to thaw.

1. Juice lime for soup recipe and follow steps 1 through 4.
2. Follow salad recipe steps 1 through 3.
3. Preheat oven to 400 degrees for enchiladas recipe and follow steps 1 through 11.
4. Follow soup recipe step 5 and serve.
5. Follow enchiladas recipe step 12 and salad recipe step 4.

RECIPES

Avocado Soup

2 medium-size avocados, chilled
2 tablespoons lime juice
1 teaspoon sugar
1 teaspoon salt
1 teaspoon ground cumin
2 cups buttermilk
Salt
Freshly ground white pepper

1. Halve avocados lengthwise. Remove and discard pits (see page 12). Cut 1 avocado half crosswise into 2 quarters. Cover one quarter with plastic wrap and refrigerate until needed. With metal spoon, scoop remaining avocado into processor fitted with metal blade or into blender.
2. Add lime juice, sugar, salt, and cumin to avocado and purée.
3. With motor still running, gradually add buttermilk. When buttermilk is totally incorporated, slowly add about 1 cup ice water. Soup should be of pourable consistency; it will thicken slightly when chilled. (Do this step in two batches if necessary.) Season with salt and pepper to taste.
4. Pour soup into 4 bowls set on baking sheet or tray, cover, and freeze until serving time, up to one-half hour. (If holding longer, refrigerate first, then freeze for one-half hour.)
5. Just before serving, peel reserved avocado quarter and slice into 8 crescents. Remove soup from freezer and float 2 crescents in each bowl.

Green Chili and Cheese Enchiladas

6 large, medium-hot, fresh green chilies, roasted, peeled, and seeded, or 6 canned chilies, rinsed, drained, and patted dry
Small head Romaine lettuce
⅓ cup coriander leaves
Small clove garlic
3 tablespoons corn oil, approximately
4 scallions
1 cup farmer cheese
1 cup sour cream
12 fresh corn tortillas, or 12 frozen tortillas, thawed
¼ pound sharp Cheddar cheese
Radishes for garnish

1. Prepare chilies (see pages 9, 10).
2. Wash lettuce and dry in salad spinner or pat dry with paper towels. Tear 4 leaves into pieces; set aside re-mainder. Wash coriander leaves and dry in salad spinner or pat dry with paper towels. Chop coarsely. Peel garlic and chop coarsely.
3. For sauce, combine torn Romaine leaves, coriander, garlic, and oil in processor fitted with metal blade or in blender and process until coarsely textured.
4. Pour one third of chili sauce into baking dish. Distribute evenly over bottom of dish.
5. Trim scallion greens and reserve whites for another use. Wash greens, pat dry with paper towels, and cut into ⅛-inch-thick rounds.
6. In small bowl, crumble farmer cheese. Combine with sour cream and half of remaining chili sauce.
7. Fill and roll tortillas: Divide farmer cheese mixture among tortillas, spooning it into long strips laid slightly off center. From the "short" sides, roll neatly into enchiladas and place them seam-side-down in baking dish.
8. Measure corn oil into small bowl. With pastry brush, baste enchiladas, being sure to coat edges as well as tops and sides. Cover dish with aluminum foil, set in upper level of 400-degree oven, and bake about 10 minutes, or until enchiladas are heated through.
9. Heat remaining chili sauce in saucepan over low heat.
10. In processor fitted with shredding blade or with grater, shred enough Cheddar cheese to measure 1½ cups, loosely packed. With chef's knife, chop reserved Romaine leaves into ⅛-inch-thick shreds. Wash and trim radishes; cut decoratively, if desired.
11. Remove baking dish from oven, uncover, and spread warmed chili sauce evenly over enchiladas. Sprinkle with grated cheese, return to oven, and bake, uncovered, 5 minutes, or until cheese has melted and sauce is bubbly.
12. With spatula, transfer 3 enchiladas to each of 4 plates. Garnish with shredded lettuce and radishes. Serve immediately.

Carrot, Apple, and Walnut Salad

1 pound carrots
2 medium-size crisp red apples, such as Winesap or Cortland (about ¾ pound total weight)
1 teaspoon granulated sugar
1 teaspoon freshly ground coriander seeds, or 1 to 2 teaspoons packaged ground coriander
¾ teaspoon salt
¼ cup cider vinegar
2 tablespoons corn oil
¼ cup walnut pieces, coarsely chopped

1. Trim and peel carrots. Shred in food processor fitted with shredding blade or with grater. Transfer to large bowl.
2. Wash and core apples; cut into quarters. Slice into thin crescents and add to carrots.
3. For dressing, blend sugar, coriander, salt, vinegar, and oil in small bowl. Pour over carrots and apples, and toss until evenly coated. Cover and chill until serving time.
4. Just before serving, add walnuts and toss. Divide among 4 bowls and serve with enchiladas.

Pineapple-Tequila Cooler
Corn Pudding with Chilies and Cheese
Zucchini and Tomato Salad with Pine Nuts

This menu works well as a buffet brunch or luncheon: Start with the iced pineapple-tequila drink, then, when the corn pudding is bubbly and brown, serve it in its baking dish with zucchini-tomato salad on the side.

Stone-ground cornmeal, which the cook prefers for the main-course pudding, is a coarse meal in which more of the nutrients of the corn kernel have been preserved. You can readily find this type of meal in health food stores and specialty food shops. Refrigerate stone-ground cornmeal in an airtight container for up to three months.

WHAT TO DRINK

Precede this meal with the cook's Pineapple-Tequila Cooler. You might then switch to the delicate fruitiness and slight sweetness of a German or a New York State Riesling.

SHOPPING LIST AND STAPLES

4 small zucchini (about 1 to 1¼ pounds total weight)
4 medium-size tomatoes (about 1½ pounds total weight)
4 medium-size ears fresh corn, or two 10-ounce packages frozen kernels
3 medium-large, medium-hot fresh green chilies, or 4-ounce can
Small bunch scallions
Small clove garlic
Small bunch basil
Small bunch parsley
Small bunch mint (optional)
3 grapefruit (about 3½ pounds total weight)
20-ounce can plus 8-ounce can pineapple chunks, in unsweetened juice
2 eggs
2¼ cups buttermilk
2 tablespoons unsalted butter
¾ pound Monterey Jack cheese or Danish Havarti
⅓ cup olive oil
2 tablespoons red wine vinegar
3 tablespoons Grenadine syrup, approximately
1 cup yellow cornmeal, preferably stone-ground
½ teaspoon sugar
2-ounce jar pine nuts
¾ teaspoon baking soda
½ teaspoon baking powder
Salt and freshly ground pepper
1¼ cups tequila, preferably gold

UTENSILS

Food processor or blender
Small skillet
Large saucepan
8 x 8 x 2-inch baking dish
Salad bowl or platter
2-quart pitcher
Large bowl
2 medium-size bowls
Colander
Medium-fine sieve
Measuring cups and spoons
Chef's knife

Paring knife
Long-handled spoon
Wooden spoon
Long, double-pronged fork
Rubber spatula
Grater
Juicer (optional)
Tongs

START-TO-FINISH STEPS

Two hours ahead: If using frozen corn for pudding recipe, set out to thaw. Refrigerate pineapple for tequila drink; squeeze grapefruit juice and refrigerate.

Thirty minutes ahead: Prepare chilies (see pages 9, 10) for corn pudding recipe.

1. Follow tequila recipe steps 1 through 4.
2. Follow salad recipe steps 1 through 5 and tequila recipe step 5.
3. Follow salad recipe steps 6 and 7.
4. Follow corn pudding recipe steps 1 through 10.
5. While corn pudding is baking, follow salad recipe steps 8 and 9, and tequila recipe step 6.
6. Follow corn pudding recipe step 11, salad recipe step 10, and serve.

RECIPES

Pineapple-Tequila Cooler

20-ounce can plus 8-ounce can pineapple chunks, in unsweetened juice
2 cups freshly squeezed grapefruit juice, chilled
1 cup tequila, preferably gold
3 tablespoons Grenadine syrup, approximately
Mint sprigs for garnish

1. In food processor fitted with metal blade or in blender, purée pineapple chunks and juice until smooth (in two batches, if necessary).
2. Transfer purée to large bowl. Stir in grapefruit juice and tequila.
3. Press mixture through sieve set over pitcher. Discard pulp.
4. Add Grenadine syrup to taste. Stir, cover, and refrigerate.
5. Wash mint sprigs, if using. Pat dry, wrap in paper towels, and refrigerate until ready to serve.
6. Pour cooler into 4 tall glasses filled with ice and serve garnished with mint sprigs.

Corn Pudding with Chilies and Cheese

4 medium-size ears fresh corn, or two 10-ounce packages frozen kernels, thawed
4 scallions
3 medium-large, medium-hot, fresh green chilies, roasted, peeled, and seeded, or 3 canned chilies, rinsed, drained, and patted dry

¾ pound Monterey Jack or Danish Havarti
1 cup yellow cornmeal, preferably stone-ground
½ teaspoon baking powder
¾ teaspoon baking soda
½ teaspoon salt
2 eggs
2¼ cups buttermilk
2 tablespoons unsalted butter

1. Place baking dish in cold oven and set oven temperature at 425 degrees.
2. While oven is heating, shuck fresh corn, if using, and trim stub of cob so that thick end will rest flat against cutting surface. To hull corn, grip corn with one hand and slice downward, following contours of cob. Rotate corn and repeat process. (You should have 1¾ to 2¼ cups kernels.)
3. Trim scallions, wash, and pat dry. Slice into ⅛-inch-thick pieces. Dice chilies.
4. Dice enough cheese to measure 1 cup and grate remainder. Set aside.
5. In large bowl, combine cornmeal, baking powder, baking soda, and salt.
6. In medium-size bowl, combine slightly beaten eggs, corn, chilies, scallions, diced cheese, and buttermilk.
7. Remove heated baking dish from oven. Melt butter in dish, rotating dish until evenly coated.
8. Immediately, pour the egg mixture into the cornmeal mixture, stirring just until combined. (Do not beat.)
9. With rubber spatula, scrape pudding into hot baking dish, top with cheese, and place in upper third of oven.
10. Bake about 25 minutes, or until golden and firm, but slightly soft in center.
11. Remove pudding from oven and serve.

Zucchini and Tomato Salad with Pine Nuts

2½ teaspoons salt
¼ cup coarsely chopped basil
2 tablespoons minced parsley plus additional sprigs for garnish (optional)
Small clove garlic
4 small zucchini (about 1 to 1¼ pounds total weight)
4 medium-size tomatoes (about 1½ pounds total weight)
¼ cup pine nuts
½ teaspoon sugar
Freshly ground pepper
2 tablespoons red wine vinegar
⅓ cup olive oil

1. Bring 2 quarts water and 2 teaspoons salt to a boil over high heat.
2. While water is heating, wash basil and parsley and pat dry with paper towels. If using parsley sprigs for garnish, wrap in paper towels and refrigerate. Coarsely chop basil and mince parsley. Peel garlic and chop coarsely.
3. Wash zucchini. Blanch in boiling water 3 to 4 minutes, or until slightly soft. Meanwhile, fill medium-size bowl with ice water.

4. Transfer zucchini to colander with tongs. Refresh under cold running water, then plunge into ice water.
5. Immerse tomatoes in pot of still boiling water. In about 1 minute, or as soon as water returns to a boil, transfer tomatoes to colander. Refresh under cold running water, then plunge into ice water with zucchini. Leave 5 minutes.
6. Drain zucchini and tomatoes and pat dry with paper towels. Slice zucchini into ⅛-inch-thick rounds. Peel and core tomatoes. Slice in half crosswise and gently squeeze out seeds. Reserve 2 halves and cut remaining tomatoes into ¼- to ½-inch-thick slices.
7. Combine tomato and zucchini slices in salad bowl or arrange on platter, cover, and refrigerate.
8. In small dry skillet, toast pine nuts over medium heat 3 to 4 minutes, or until fragrant and lightly browned. Set aside.
9. In food processor fitted with metal blade or in blender, purée reserved tomato halves, remaining ½ teaspoon salt, sugar, pepper, basil, parsley, garlic, and vinegar. With motor running, add olive oil in a slow, steady stream and process, until mixture is thick and smooth. Set aside.
10. Just before serving, beat dressing to recombine, pour over salad, sprinkle with pine nuts, and garnish with parsley sprigs, if desired.

ADDED TOUCH

This refreshingly light gelatin dessert is made with fresh fruit juices.

Citrus Gelatin

½ cup granulated sugar
2 envelopes unflavored gelatin
2 small grapefruit
2 medium-size juice oranges
1 lemon
Few drops red and yellow food coloring (optional)
Four orange slices, decoratively cut, for garnish (optional)

1. Combine sugar, gelatin, and 1½ cups cold water in medium-size saucepan. Do not stir.
2. Wash 1 grapefruit and 1 orange, and pat dry with paper towels. Cut thin strips of rind, avoiding white pith. Add strips of rind to saucepan with gelatin.
3. Halve oranges and grapefruit, and squeeze enough juice to measure 1½ cups combined. Halve lemon and squeeze ¼ cup juice. Add juices to saucepan.
4. Simmer mixture, stirring constantly, about 5 minutes, or until mixture becomes clear.
5. Strain mixture through fine sieve set over bowl. Discard solids and rinse sieve. If desired, add very small amount of food coloring to mixture. Set sieve over serving bowl and strain mixture again.
6. Cover and refrigerate at least 3 hours, or until completely set.
7. Spoon into individual goblets or bowls and serve garnished with orange slices, if desired.

Sue B. Huffman

MENU 1 (Left)
Chicken Breasts with Sour Cream and Jalapeños
Green Rice
Jerusalem Artichoke and Orange Salad

MENU 2
Chicken Soup with Tortilla Strips
Mexican Corn Bread
Chorizo with Zucchini

MENU 3
Tamale Pie with Green Sauce
Tossed Green Salad with Papaya

For Sue Huffman, cooking has been a lifelong avocation; she learned to cook when she was five. Now a magazine food editor, she describes herself as a home-style cook who prefers unadorned one-course or one-pot meals without any heavy sauces and frills. Her interest in Tex-Mex and Mexican foods stems from her Oklahoma childhood ("I grew up eating Tex-Mex," she says) and from her stay in southern California, where she became acquainted with both Cal-Mex and genuine Mexican cuisines. She also learned to value fresh herbs, particularly coriander, a featured ingredient in several of her recipes.

In Menu 1, chopped coriander flavors the sour-cream-based spread for the chicken breasts and colors the accompanying rice. She uses chopped coriander again for both color and flavor in the chicken soup of Menu 2.

The tamale pie in Menu 3 has an unusual crust made of *masa harina*—Mexican corn flour—rather than the standard yellow cornmeal. Perfect for an informal supper, the tamale pie is accompanied by a lettuce and papaya salad.

Chicken "cutlets"—topped with a mixture of sour cream, grated cheese, and chopped chilies—comprise the main course which is complemented by "green" rice with chopped coriander and parsley and a side salad of orange, onion, and Jerusalem artichoke slices arranged on lettuce leaves.

37

Chicken Breasts with Sour Cream and Jalapeños
Green Rice
Jerusalem Artichoke and Orange Salad

Boned, skinned turkey breasts, or scallops, are good substitutes for chicken. Most supermarkets package fresh turkey scallops, but, if your market stocks only whole breasts, ask the butcher to prepare them for you. If you cannot find fresh coriander for the sour-cream topping, omit it; seeds or dried flakes are not a suitable substitute here.

Despite their name, Jerusalem artichokes, or sunchokes, are not related to green-globe artichokes. They are the knobby root of a type of sunflower. Eaten raw, they have the texture of water chestnuts and a slightly sweet, nutty flavor. Many supermarkets and health-food stores stock them. Refrigerated in a tightly closed plastic bag, they will keep for a week or two. If available, jícama is a worthy substitute.

WHAT TO DRINK

A crisp, dry white wine, like a French Muscadet, an Italian Verdicchio, or a California Sauvignon Blanc, works very well with the bright flavors of this menu. A full-bodied amber ale also would be satisfactory.

SHOPPING LIST AND STAPLES

4 whole chicken breasts, boned, skinned, and pounded to ¼- to ½-inch thickness (about 1½ pounds total weight)
2 Jerusalem artichokes (about ½ pound total weight)
Small head Romaine lettuce
1 to 2 fresh jalapeños, or 4-ounce can
Medium-size red onion
Small white onion
2 cloves garlic
Large bunch parsley
Large bunch coriander
2 navel oranges
2 limes
½ pint sour cream
1 tablespoon unsalted butter
¼ pound Monterey Jack cheese
2½ cups chicken stock, preferably homemade (see page 13) or canned
3 tablespoons vegetable oil
1 tablespoon honey
1½ cups long-grain rice
Dash of ground coriander seed
Salt and freshly ground pepper

UTENSILS

Food processor or blender
Electric mixer
Large heavy-gauge skillet
Medium-size saucepan with cover
Broiler tray
Medium-size bowl
2 small bowls
Colander
Salad spinner (optional)
Measuring cups and spoons
Chef's knife
Paring knife
Wooden spoon
Metal spatula
Rubber spatula (optional)
Grater
Juicer (optional)

START-TO-FINISH STEPS

1. Follow rice recipe step 1.
2. While water is heating, wash coriander and parsley for chicken and rice recipes; pat dry, trim stems, and chop 2 tablespoons coriander for chicken recipe. Peel onions; quarter white onion for rice recipe and thinly slice red onion for salad recipe. Peel garlic for rice recipe.
3. Follow rice recipe steps 2 and 3.
4. While rice is soaking, follow salad recipe steps 1 through 6.
5. Follow rice recipe steps 4 through 6.
6. While rice is cooking, follow chicken recipe steps 1 through 3.
7. Follow rice recipe step 7.
8. Follow chicken recipe steps 4 through 6.
9. Follow chicken recipe step 7, rice recipe step 8, and serve with salad.

RECIPES

Chicken Breasts with Sour Cream and Jalapeños

1 to 2 fresh jalapeños, or 4-ounce can
¼ pound Monterey Jack cheese
2 tablespoons chopped coriander
½ cup sour cream

4 whole chicken breasts, boned, skinned, and pounded to
  ¼- to ½-inch thickness (about 1½ pounds total weight)
Salt
Freshly ground pepper
1 tablespoon unsalted butter
1 tablespoon vegetable oil

1. If using fresh jalapeños, wash and pat dry; seed and
derib, if desired. If using canned, rinse, drain, and pat
dry. Chop chilies.
2. Shred enough cheese to measure ¼ cup. In small bowl,
combine cheese with chilies, chopped coriander, and sour
cream. Set aside.
3. Preheat broiler. Line broiler tray with aluminum foil
and set aside.
4. Sprinkle both sides of chicken breasts with salt and
pepper to taste.
5. Combine butter and oil in large heavy-gauge skillet
over medium-high heat. Sauté chicken breasts, 2 at a time,
about 5 minutes per side, or until brown. Transfer to
broiler tray.
6. Top each chicken breast with a generous spoonful of
sour-cream mixture. Broil 4 to 5 inches from heating element about 5 minutes, or until topping bubbles.
7. Transfer to platter and serve immediately.

Green Rice

1½ cups long-grain rice
¼ cup plus 2 tablespoons coriander leaves, tightly packed
½ cup parsley leaves, tightly packed
Small white onion, quartered
2 cloves garlic, peeled
2½ cups chicken stock
2 tablespoons vegetable oil
Salt
Freshly ground pepper

1. Bring 1 quart water to a boil over high heat.
2. Combine rice with boiling water to cover in medium-
size bowl. Stir once and set aside to soak 15 minutes.
3. In food processor fitted with steel blade, chop coriander, parsley, onion, and garlic. Add ¼ cup chicken stock
and purée. Or, with chef's knife, finely chop coriander,
parsley, onion, and garlic; then place in blender, add stock,
and purée. Set aside.
4. Transfer soaked rice to colander. Rinse under cold running water and drain.
5. Heat oil in medium-size saucepan over high heat. Add
rice and sauté, stirring, about 5 minutes, or until
translucent.
6. Reduce heat to medium. Stir in coriander-parsley mixture and cook, stirring frequently, about 10 minutes, or
until fairly dry.
7. Add the remaining stock and salt and pepper to taste.
Bring to a boil over high heat, stir once, reduce to a
simmer, and cover. Cook 15 minutes, or until rice is just
tender and stock is absorbed.
8. Turn rice into serving bowl.

Jerusalem Artichoke and Orange Salad

8 leaves Romaine lettuce
2 navel oranges
2 Jerusalem artichokes
1 cup sliced red onion, approximately
2 limes
1 tablespoon honey
Dash of ground coriander seed

1. Wash lettuce leaves; dry in salad spinner or pat dry with
paper towels.
2. Peel oranges and cut into ¼-inch-thick rounds.
3. Peel artichokes and cut into ¼-inch-thick pieces.
4. Arrange lettuce leaves on individual serving plates.
Top with alternating slices of orange and artichoke.
5. Separate onion slices into rings and scatter over salads.
6. Squeeze enough lime to measure ¼ cup juice. Combine
with honey and ground coriander in small bowl; beat until
blended. Spoon dressing over salad, cover, and refrigerate
until ready to serve.

ADDED TOUCH

If you wish, you can prepare this rich mousse a day ahead.
Coffee-flavored liqueur and brewed coffee intensify the
flavor.

Chocolate Kahlúa Mousse

4 ounces semisweet chocolate
2 tablespoons strong coffee
3 large eggs
3 tablespoons Kahlúa
1 teaspoon vanilla extract
1 cup heavy cream

1. In freezer, chill medium-size bowl and beaters for whip-
ping cream.
2. Meanwhile, break chocolate into pieces, combine with
coffee in small, heavy-gauge saucepan, and melt, stirring,
over very low heat.
3. Separate eggs, yolks into small bowl and whites into
medium-size bowl.
4. With wire whisk, beat yolks. Gradually whisk a small
amount of chocolate mixture into yolks; then, over very
low heat, whisk yolk mixture back into remaining chocolate mixture. Stir just until combined. Remove from heat
and stir in Kahlúa and vanilla. Set aside to cool.
5. In chilled bowl, whip cream with electric mixer until
stiff but not buttery. Wash and dry beaters.
6. Beat whites at low speed until foamy. Increase speed to
medium and beat until stiff peaks form.
7. With rubber spatula, fold about one third of whites into
cooled chocolate mixture. Add remaining whites, folding
in gently but thoroughly.
8. Add whipped cream to egg white-chocolate mixture,
folding gently but thoroughly.
9. Turn mixture into 1-quart serving dish. Cover and refrigerate at least 4 hours or overnight.
10. Spoon into individual bowls or goblets and serve.

Chicken Soup with Tortilla Strips
Mexican Corn Bread
Chorizo with Zucchini

This filling meal can be as mild or as spicy as you like, depending on the kind and quantity of chilies you use and the sausage you select. The chicken soup, a flavorful blend of spices, gains richness from the chicken breast-bones, which you simmer in stock until the meat is tender.

WHAT TO DRINK

Almost any kind of beer is right with this menu, but, when fresh peaches are in season, consider a pitcher of sangria.

SHOPPING LIST AND STAPLES

1 whole chicken breast (about 1½ pounds), skinned and split
3 mild or hot chorizo or Italian sausages (½ to ¾ pound total weight)
3 medium-size zucchini (about 1 pound total weight)
Small bunch carrots (with tops, optional)
Small bunch celery (if not using carrot tops)
1 to 2 fresh jalapeños, plus one additional (optional), or 4-ounce can
Small onion
3 cloves garlic
Medium-size bunch coriander
Small avocado
2 to 3 limes
1 egg
½ pint sour cream
¼ pound sharp Cheddar cheese
6 fresh corn tortillas, or 1 package frozen
8 cups chicken stock, preferably homemade (see page 13) or five 13¾-ounce cans
8-ounce can creamed corn
8-ounce can tomato sauce
4-ounce can mild green chilies
6 tablespoons vegetable oil
½ cup yellow cornmeal
2 teaspoons baking powder
Salt and freshly ground pepper

UTENSILS

Large skillet
Medium-size skillet
Large saucepan with cover
8 x 8 x 2-inch baking dish
Plate

A wedge of corn bread baked with jalapeño chilies accompanies the main-course chicken soup garnished with avocado slices. Stir-fried chorizo sausage and zucchini is a substantial side dish.

Large bowl
2 medium-size bowls
Colander
Measuring cups and spoons
Chef's knife
Paring knife
Wooden spoon
Fork
Metal wok spatula or slotted spoon
Whisk
Vegetable peeler (optional)
Ladle
Grater
Juicer (optional)

START-TO-FINISH STEPS

One hour ahead: If using frozen tortillas for chicken soup recipe, set out to thaw.

1. Follow corn bread recipe step 1.
2. Follow chicken soup recipe step 1.
3. While soup is simmering, follow corn bread recipe steps 2 through 6.
4. While corn bread is baking, follow soup recipe steps 2 and 3, and chorizo recipe step 1.
5. Follow corn bread recipe step 7 and soup recipe steps 4 and 5.
6. Follow chorizo recipe step 2.
7. While chorizo is browning, follow soup recipe step 6.
8. While soup is simmering, follow chorizo recipe step 3.
9. Follow soup recipe step 7, chorizo recipe step 4, and serve with corn bread.

RECIPES

Chicken Soup with Tortilla Strips

Medium-size carrot, peeled and halved crosswise
Small bunch carrot or celery tops
9 sprigs coriander
Small onion, peeled and quartered
1 whole chicken breast (about 1¼ pounds), skinned and split
Medium-size clove garlic, peeled and crushed
Freshly ground pepper
8 cups chicken stock
6 fresh or frozen corn tortillas
3 tablespoons vegetable oil
Small avocado
½ cup tomato sauce
2 tablespoons freshly squeezed lime juice
1 to 2 jalapeño chilies, seeded and quartered
Salt

1. Combine carrot, celery or carrot tops, 6 sprigs of coriander, onion, chicken breast, garlic, pepper to taste, and stock in large saucepan and bring to a boil over medium-high heat. Reduce heat and simmer, covered, about 25 minutes, or until chicken is tender.

2. Line plate with paper towels. Cut tortillas into ½-inch-wide strips. Heat oil in medium-size skillet over medium-high heat until it shimmers. Add tortilla strips and fry, stirring constantly, about 2 minutes, or until golden. Transfer to paper-towel-lined plate.
3. Strain soup into large bowl. Refrigerate chicken, uncovered. Return strained broth to saucepan; set aside.
4. Ten minutes before serving, bring soup to a simmer over medium-high heat.
5. Peel, halve, and pit avocado. Cut crosswise into ½- to ¾-inch-thick slices. Set aside.
6. Bone cooled chicken breast and shred meat. Add shredded meat, tortilla strips, tomato sauce, lime juice, remaining coriander sprigs, and jalapeño quarters to soup and stir. Simmer 5 minutes.
7. Add salt and freshly ground pepper to taste, ladle into individual bowls, and serve garnished with avocado slices.

Mexican Corn Bread

½ cup yellow cornmeal
2 teaspoons baking powder
¼ teaspoon salt
1 egg
3 tablespoons vegetable oil
½ cup sour cream
1 cup creamed corn
1 cup shredded sharp Cheddar cheese
¼ cup canned chopped mild green chilies
½ fresh jalapeño, seeded and chopped (optional)

1. Preheat oven to 400 degrees.
2. Lightly grease baking dish.
3. Combine dry ingredients in medium-size bowl.
4. In another medium-size bowl, lightly beat egg. Beat in oil, then sour cream. Stir in creamed corn and shredded cheese.
5. Pour corn mixture into cornmeal mixture. Add chilies, and jalapeño, if using. Stir just until combined.
6. Turn into greased baking dish and bake 25 minutes, or until corn bread is puffed and golden brown.
7. Remove corn bread from oven. Cut into squares, cover loosely with foil, and keep warm until serving time.

Chorizo with Zucchini

3 mild or hot chorizo or Italian sausages
3 medium-size zucchini (about 1 pound total weight)
2 cloves garlic, peeled and crushed
1 to 2 teaspoons freshly squeezed lime juice
Salt

1. Cut chorizo or Italian sausages crosswise into ¼- to ½-inch-thick slices. Rinse zucchini, pat dry, and cut crosswise into ¼-inch-thick slices.
2. Sauté chorizo in large skillet over medium-high heat about 5 minutes, or until browned.
3. Add zucchini and garlic, and stir fry about 5 minutes, or until zucchini is barely tender.
4. Stir in lime juice, add salt to taste, and turn into serving bowl.

Tamale Pie with Green Sauce
Tossed Green Salad with Papaya

Tomatoes and scallions decorate the tamale pie, which is accompanied by a salad of lettuce and papaya with lime-juice dressing.

Tamales are corn flour (*masa harina*) dough, with or without filling, baked in cornhusks. Here, the main-dish tamale pie is a simple variation on the original tamale. The dough, in this instance a pie crust, is covered with seasoned ground beef and melted cheese and topped with scallions and tomatoes. The green sauce served with the pie contains tomatillos and fresh coriander.

WHAT TO DRINK

Try a robust red wine here: either a California Zinfandel or an Italian Dolcetto.

SHOPPING LIST AND STAPLES

1 pound ground beef
Medium-size head Romaine lettuce
2 medium-size tomatoes (about 1 pound total weight)
Medium-size bunch scallions
Medium-size onion, plus 1 small
1 large and 2 medium-size cloves garlic
Small bunch coriander
1 to 2 fresh jalapeños, or 4-ounce can
Small papaya
1 to 2 limes

½ pound Cheddar cheese, approximately
½ pint sour cream
13-ounce can tomatillos
¼ cup plus 2 tablespoons vegetable oil
1¼ cups masa harina
2 tablespoons chili powder
1 tablespoon plus a dash of ground cumin
Dash of oregano
Salt and freshly ground pepper

UTENSILS

Food processor or blender
Large skillet
9-inch pie plate
3 small bowls
Measuring cups and spoons
Chef's knife
Paring knife
Wooden spoon
Fork
Metal spatula or pie server
Rubber spatula
Grater
Juicer
Garlic press

START-TO-FINISH STEPS

1. Follow tamale pie recipe steps 1 through 4.
2. Follow sauce recipe steps 1 and 2.
3. Follow salad recipe step 1.
4. Follow tamale pie recipe steps 5 and 6.
5. Follow salad recipe step 2.
6. Follow tamale recipe step 7, sauce recipe step 3, salad recipe step 3, and serve.

RECIPES

Tamale Pie with Green Sauce

Crust:
1¼ cups masa harina
2 tablespoons vegetable oil
¾ teaspoon salt

Filling:
1 pound ground beef
1 cup chopped onion
Large clove garlic, peeled and pressed
2 tablespoons chili powder
1 tablespoon ground cumin
Dash of oregano
Salt and freshly ground pepper
1½ cups shredded sharp Cheddar cheese

Topping:
1 bunch scallions
2 medium-size tomatoes
Green Sauce (see following recipe)

1. Preheat oven to 400 degrees.
2. Combine masa harina, ⅔ cup water, oil, and salt in 9-inch pie plate, and stir with fork until blended. With your fingers, pat crust evenly onto bottom and sides of pie plate. Bake 10 minutes or until crust is lightly golden.
3. For filling, sauté beef in large skillet over medium heat, stirring with fork to break up lumps, about 5 minutes, or until fat is rendered. Add onion and garlic, and sauté, stirring, about 5 minutes, or until soft. Remove crust from oven and set aside.
4. Drain fat, return pan to heat, and stir in chili powder, cumin, oregano, and salt and pepper to taste. Sauté, stirring, 7 to 8 minutes, or until beef is brown. Set aside.
5. Turn beef mixture into crust, sprinkle with cheese, and bake about 5 minutes, or just until cheese melts.
6. While pie is baking, prepare topping: Wash scallions, pat dry, trim, and chop. Wash tomatoes and pat dry. Core, halve, seed, and dice.
7. Remove pie from oven, heap scallions in center and surround with tomatoes. Serve with Green Sauce.

Green Sauce

1 to 2 fresh or canned jalapeños
13-ounce can tomatillos with liquid
Small onion, peeled and halved
Medium-size clove garlic, peeled and crushed
2 tablespoons chopped coriander
Salt
¾ cup sour cream

1. If using fresh jalapeños, wash and pat dry; seed and derib, if desired. If using canned, rinse, drain, and pat dry. Chop chilies.
2. In food processor fitted with steel blade or in blender, purée tomatillos, onion, garlic, chilies, coriander, and salt to taste. Turn into small bowl, cover, and refrigerate.
3. Just before serving, blend sour cream into sauce and taste for seasoning.

Tossed Green Salad with Papaya

4 teaspoons freshly squeezed lime juice
Dash of ground cumin
Medium-size clove garlic, peeled and crushed
¼ cup vegetable oil
Salt and freshly ground pepper
8 to 10 leaves Romaine lettuce
Small papaya

1. Combine lime juice, cumin, and garlic in small bowl. Beat in vegetable oil and add salt and pepper to taste.
2. Wash Romaine and dry in salad spinner or pat dry with paper towels. Tear into bite-sized pieces. Peel papaya, halve lengthwise, scoop out seeds, and discard. Cut into ½-inch cubes. Combine Romaine and papaya in salad bowl.
3. Just before serving, stir dressing to recombine and remove garlic. Add dressing to salad and toss.

Barbara Hansen

MENU 1 (Left)
Mexican Corn Soup
Steak Salad
Bananas with Custard Sauce

MENU 2
Sliced Papayas with Lime Wedges
Scrambled Eggs with Shrimp
Quesadillas

MENU 3
Shrimp Guacamole
Pork Cutlets with Tomato Sauce
Mexican-Style Vermicelli

L ong a devotee of Mexican cooking, Barbara Hansen has studied her subject in Mexico as well as in Los Angeles, which has a large Mexican population and many Mexican groceries and markets.

Her three menus draw from many regional styles, including that of California. The main-course steak salad in Menu 1 was inspired by a meal in a Los Angeles café. It reflects the California influence: broiled strips of steak, mashed avocado, grated cheese, and sour cream. The light corn soup comes from the south of Mexico, and the bananas with custard sauce recreates a dessert from Puerto Vallarta on the Pacific coast.

Menus 2 and 3 are classic Mexican fare. An informal brunch, Menu 2 features a papaya and lime fruit platter, followed by scrambled eggs and shrimp, an adaptation of a northern dish that calls for shredded cooked beef. *Quesadillas* (toasted or fried tortilla turnovers) accompany the eggs. Sautéed pork cutlets with a lightly seasoned tomato sauce are the main dish in Menu 3, a company dinner. The pork and its vermicelli side dish look Italian, yet both are favorites throughout Mexico. The addition of shrimp turns the accompanying *guacamole* into a substantial appetizer.

Individual bowls of corn soup with a coriander garnish can be served as a side dish or an appetizer. Layer the components of the steak salad on a plate, then make a border around the salad with fried tortilla triangles, pinwheel style. Arrange the bananas and custard cream on bright plates, and serve a pitcher of well-iced sangria with slices of apple and orange.

Mexican Corn Soup
Steak Salad
Bananas with Custard Sauce

The broiled steak cubes for the main-course salad can be served hot or at room temperature. If you wish, you can make portions of this salad ahead: Prepare the avocado topping, grate the cheese, shred the lettuce, then refrigerate. You can also deep fry the tortilla triangles well ahead of time and store them in an airtight container to keep them crisp.

WHAT TO DRINK

The cook suggests serving margaritas before dinner, sangria with the meal, and Mexican coffee with dessert.

SHOPPING LIST AND STAPLES

1½ pounds sirloin tip, top sirloin, or flank steak, ¾ to 1 inch thick
2 ears corn, or 10-ounce package frozen kernels
Large avocado
Small head Iceberg lettuce (about 1 pound)
Medium-size tomato (4 to 6 ounces)
Medium-size onion
Small bunch scallions
1 fresh jalapeño, or 4-ounce can
2 medium-size cloves garlic
Medium-size bunch coriander or parsley
1 lime
4 medium-size bananas
1 egg
1¼ cups milk
½ pint sour cream
1 tablespoon unsalted butter
¼ pound Monterey Jack cheese
¼ pound Longhorn Cheddar cheese
6 fresh 6-inch corn tortillas, or 1 package frozen
3 cups chicken stock, preferably homemade (see page 13), or canned
1 cup vegetable oil, approximately
2 tablespoons white wine vinegar
¾ teaspoon vanilla extract
2 to 3 tablespoons sugar
2 teaspoons cornstarch
¼ teaspoon oregano
Dash of cinnamon
Dash of cumin
Salt
½ teaspoon cracked black pepper

UTENSILS

Food processor or blender
Medium-size skillet
Medium-size saucepan with cover
Small saucepan
Broiler pan
Platter
Cutting board
Salad spinner (optional)
Fine mesh sieve
Large bowl
2 medium-size bowls
2 small bowls, plus one additional (if not using jar)
Small jar with lid or small bowl
Measuring cups and spoons
Chef's knife
Paring knife
Wooden spoon
Metal spoon
Fork
Tongs
Mortar and pestle
Grater (if not using processor)

START-TO-FINISH STEPS

One-hour ahead: If using frozen tortillas for steak salad, set out to thaw.

1. Follow bananas recipe steps 1 through 5.
2. Follow salad recipe steps 1 through 7.
3. Follow soup recipe steps 1 through 4.
4. Follow salad recipe steps 8 through 10.
5. Follow soup recipe steps 5 and 6.
6. Follow salad recipe steps 11 through 16.
7. Follow soup recipe step 7 and serve with steak salad.
8. For dessert, follow bananas recipe steps 6 and 7, and serve.

RECIPES

Mexican Corn Soup

2 ears corn, or 10-ounce package frozen kernels
1 tablespoon unsalted butter
Medium-size onion, peeled and finely chopped
¼ to ½ jalapeño, seeded and finely chopped

1 tablespoon chopped coriander or parsley, plus additional sprigs for garnish (optional)
3 cups chicken stock
½ teaspoon salt

1. If using fresh corn, shuck and trim stub of cob so that thick end will rest flat against cutting board. To hull, grip corn with one hand and slice downward, following contours of cob. Rotate corn and repeat process until you have 1¼ cups kernels. Or measure out 1¼ cups frozen corn kernels.
2. In medium-size saucepan, melt butter over medium heat. Add onion and sauté, stirring frequently, 5 to 6 minutes, or until tender.
3. Combine half the corn, the jalapeño, the coriander, and 1 cup chicken stock in bowl of food processor fitted with metal blade or in blender and process until finely ground.
4. Add corn mixture and remaining 2 cups stock to saucepan and bring slowly to a boil over medium heat. Reduce heat and simmer, covered, 15 minutes.
5. Strain soup through fine mesh sieve set over medium-size bowl, pressing out as much liquid as possible from the corn mixture. Discard solids left in sieve.
6. Return strained soup to saucepan and add remaining corn kernels and salt. Bring to a boil over medium heat, reduce to a simmer, and cook, covered, an additional 20 minutes. Taste for seasoning and add more salt, if needed.
7. Ladle soup into 4 individual bowls and serve garnished with sprigs of coriander or parsley, if desired.

Steak Salad

Large avocado
¼ cup chopped scallions
1 teaspoon lime juice
1½ teaspoons salt
1 head Iceberg lettuce (about 1 pound)
1½ pounds sirloin tip, top sirloin, or flank steak
2 medium-size cloves garlic
1 cup vegetable oil, approximately
½ teaspoon cracked black pepper
6 fresh corn tortillas, or 6 frozen tortillas, thawed
2 tablespoons white wine vinegar
¼ teaspoon oregano, crumbled
Dash of cumin
2 ounces Monterey Jack cheese
2 ounces Longhorn Cheddar cheese
2 medium-size tomatoes
½ cup sour cream

1. Halve avocado lengthwise. Remove and discard pit (see page 12). Scoop out flesh and place in medium-size bowl. Mash avocado with fork.
2. Combine scallions, lime juice, and ¼ teaspoon salt with avocado. Cover with plastic wrap and refrigerate.
3. Shred enough lettuce to measure 8 cups. Place in large bowl, cover, and refrigerate until needed.
4. Trim excess fat from steak and place steak on foil-lined broiler pan.

5. Peel garlic. Combine garlic and remaining teaspoon salt in mortar and mash with pestle into a paste.
6. Drizzle 1 teaspoon oil over one side of steak and evenly spread with half of garlic paste and half of pepper. Turn steak over and repeat on other side.
7. Preheat broiler.
8. Stack tortillas and cut in half. Cut each half into 3 triangles, forming 36 triangles in all.
9. Line platter with paper towels. Fill medium-size skillet ½ inch deep with oil and heat over medium-high heat until oil begins to smoke. Fry tortilla triangles in batches, about 2 to 3 minutes each, or until triangles are light brown and crisp. With tongs, transfer tortillas to platter and continue until all the triangles have been fried.
10. In small bowl or small jar with lid, combine ¼ cup oil, vinegar, ¼ teaspoon salt, oregano, and cumin. Beat well with fork or cover jar and shake well. Set aside.
11. Place meat on broiler rack 5 inches from heating element and broil 5 minutes. Turn meat with tongs and broil another 3 minutes.
12. While meat is broiling, shred cheeses in food processor or with grater and set aside.
13. Core, halve, seed, and cut tomatoes into ½-inch dice.
14. Transfer steak to cutting board. Cut into ½-inch-thick strips and then cut strips crosswise into ½-inch dice.
15. Toss lettuce with dressing. Divide lettuce among 4 dinner plates and top with steak. Place a dollop of sour cream and a dollop of avocado mixture next to each other on top of steak. Sprinkle with shredded cheeses and top with diced tomato.
16. Arrange a border of tortilla triangles on the rim of each plate and serve.

Bananas with Custard Sauce

1 egg yolk
1¼ cups milk
2 to 3 tablespoons sugar
2 teaspoons cornstarch
Dash of salt
¾ teaspoon vanilla extract
4 medium-size bananas
Cinnamon

1. In small bowl, beat yolk and gradually blend in milk.
2. Combine sugar, cornstarch, and salt in small saucepan.
3. Add a small amount of egg-milk mixture to sugar mixture and stir until smooth. Blend in remaining egg-milk mixture.
4. Bring custard sauce to a boil over medium heat, stirring constantly. Reduce to a simmer and cook, stirring, until mixture thickens slightly and coats a metal spoon, about 2 minutes.
5. Remove pan from heat and stir in vanilla. Turn sauce into small bowl, cover, and refrigerate.
6. Just before serving, peel bananas. Cut each half crosswise and then lengthwise, making 4 pieces. Divide among 4 dessert plates.
7. Spoon sauce over bananas and sprinkle with cinnamon.

Sliced Papayas with Lime Wedges
Scrambled Eggs with Shrimp
Quesadillas

Serve this brunch as a buffet: scrambled eggs with shrimp in a shallow dish, papaya slices and lime wedges on a platter, and cheese-filled tortillas in a pottery bowl. Offer a plate of flour tortillas on the side.

48

Quesadillas always contain cheese—in this recipe, grated Monterey Jack—but they can also include chilies, cooked *chorizo*, diced baked ham, sautéed mushrooms, or any combination thereof. An optional seasoning is *epazote,* a pungent herb also known as wormseed or Mexican tea, which has pointed leaves on a long stalk. Omit the fresh *epazote* if you cannot find it; there is no substitute.

WHAT TO DRINK

Beer complements this brunch menu nicely, but a screwdriver—either the classic version with vodka and orange juice or a Latin-style version with tequila—is a real eye opener.

SHOPPING LIST AND STAPLES

1 pound medium-size shrimp
2 small tomatoes (about ½ pound total weight)
2 fresh mild green chilies, or 4-ounce can
2 fresh serrano chilies or any other type of hot chili, or
    4-ounce can
Small onion
Small bunch epazote (optional)
2 large limes
2 large papayas
4 eggs
½ pound Monterey Jack cheese
4 fresh 8-inch flour tortillas, or 1 package frozen
3 tablespoons vegetable oil, approximately
Salt

UTENSILS

Food processor or grater
Large, heavy-gauge griddle or skillet
2 serving platters, medium-size skillet, preferably
    nonstick
Small bowl
Colander
Measuring cups and spoons
Chef's knife
Paring knife
Wooden spoon
Metal spatula
Kitchen shears

START-TO-FINISH STEPS

1. Prepare chilies for eggs with shrimp and quesadillas (see pages 9, 10).
2. Follow papayas recipe step 1.
3. While papayas are chilling, follow quesadillas recipe steps 1 through 7.
4. Follow eggs with shrimp recipe steps 1 through 10.
5. Follow papayas recipe steps 2 and 3, quesadillas recipe step 8, and serve with eggs.

RECIPES

Sliced Papayas with Lime Wedges

2 large papayas
2 large limes

1. Halve papayas lengthwise. Scoop out seeds and discard. Cut each half lengthwise into 4 wedges. Peel each wedge and place on platter. Cover with plastic wrap and refrigerate.
2. Just before serving, halve limes lengthwise and cut into wedges.
3. Remove papaya from refrigerator and serve garnished with lime wedges.

Scrambled Eggs with Shrimp

Small onion
2 small tomatoes
2 fresh serrano chilies or any other type of hot chili
    roasted, peeled, and seeded, or 2 canned chilies,
    rinsed, drained, and patted dry
1 pound medium-size shrimp
1 tablespoon vegetable oil
1 teaspoon salt
4 eggs

1. Peel and chop onion.
2. Wash tomatoes and pat dry. Core, halve, and seed tomatoes. Cut into ½-inch dice and set aside.
3. Cut chilies crosswise into ⅛- to ¼-inch-thick slices.
4. Pinch off legs of shrimp, several at a time, then bend back and snap off sharp, beaklike piece of shell just above tail. Remove shell and discard. Using sharp paring knife, make shallow incision along back of each shrimp, exposing black digestive vein. Extract black vein and discard (see following illustrations).

49

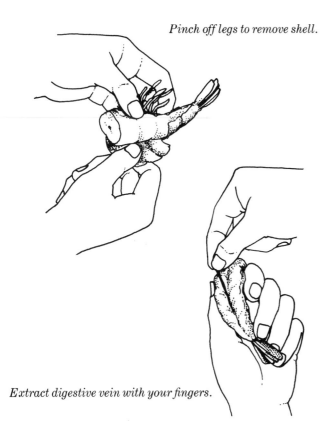

Pinch off legs to remove shell.

Extract digestive vein with your fingers.

5. Place shrimp in colander, rinse under cold running water, drain, and pat dry with paper towels. Set aside.

6. In medium-size skillet, preferably nonstick, heat oil over medium-high heat. Add onion, tomatoes, and chilies, and cook, stirring, just until heated through, about 45 seconds. Place platter in oven to warm.

7. Lower heat to medium and add shrimp and salt. Cook, stirring occasionally, until shrimp have turned pink, about 4 minutes.

8. Push shrimp mixture to one side of skillet. Crack eggs and gently drop into cleared side of skillet. Cook until eggs have just begun to set, 1 to 2 minutes.

9. Stir eggs and shrimp mixture together and continue cooking until eggs are firm, about 1 minute.

10. Turn mixture out onto warm serving platter.

Quesadillas

½ pound Monterey Jack cheese
2 fresh mild green chilies, roasted, peeled, and seeded, or
  2 canned, rinsed, drained, and patted dry

1 to 2 tablespoons oil
Four fresh or frozen 8-inch flour tortillas
Leaves from 2 sprigs epazote (optional)

1. Preheat oven to 250 degrees.
2. In food processor or with grater, shred cheese.
3. Chop chilies; set aside.
4. Heat large, heavy-gauge griddle or large heavy-gauge skillet over medium-high heat.
5. Pour 1 to 2 tablespoons oil onto griddle or skillet and tilt to coat.
6. Depending on size of griddle or skillet, place one or more tortillas flat on cooking surface. Top one half of each tortilla with one quarter of the cheese, 1 tablespoon of the chilies, and, if using, a few epazote leaves. Fold free half of tortilla over cheese and chilies, and gently pat down into place. Cook quesadillas, turning once, until cheese is melted, about 2 minutes.
7. As they are done, transfer quesadillas to serving platter and place in warm oven. Repeat until all quesadillas are cooked. Cover platter loosely with aluminum foil and leave in warm oven until ready to serve.
8. When ready to serve, remove quesadillas from oven and, with kitchen shears, cut each quesadilla into 3 triangles.

ADDED TOUCH

Atole, a Mexican version of hot cocoa, is drunk at breakfast or as a snack.

Atole

6 tablespoons rice flour, masa, or cornstarch
3 to 4 tablespoons firmly packed dark brown sugar
3 to 4 tablespoons granulated sugar
Dash of salt
2 cups milk
2 sticks cinnamon
Ground cinnamon (optional)

1. Combine rice flour, brown and granulated sugars, and salt in medium-size saucepan. Gradually add 2 cups water, stirring until mixture is smooth. Stir in milk and cinnamon sticks.
2. Bring to a boil over medium heat, stirring frequently.
3. Boil 2 minutes, stirring constantly.
4. Remove cinnamon sticks and pour atole into mugs. Sprinkle with ground cinnamon, if desired.

Shrimp Guacamole
Pork Cutlets with Tomato Sauce
Mexican-Style Vermicelli

A shrimp guacamole appetizer, sautéed pork cutlets, and vermicelli make an elegant company dinner.

For the pork cutlets, use boned center-cut chops or thinly sliced boneless pork, pounded thin. If you pound the meat at home, a wooden mallet is the best tool, but the flat side of a small skillet will also do.

This unusual *guacamole* (mashed avocado) appetizer contains chopped shrimp. You can peel, devein, and boil them the night before, then refrigerate them in an airtight container. If you have no food processor or blender, you can chop the ingredients by hand and mash the avocado with a fork. The acid in the lime juice not only enhances the avocado flavor but also preserves its color.

Mexicans sometimes serve a separate pasta course at traditional meals, such as this spicy vermicelli side dish. A thin spaghetti-like pasta, vermicelli is lightly sautéed before being simmered in stock and is ready when all the liquid is absorbed. The cooking time may vary depending on the brand of the pasta you use.

WHAT TO DRINK

The flavors of this menu will respond well to a fruity, reasonably soft red wine. A good choice would be a California Gamay Beaujolais or a young Italian Chianti or Barbera. Dark beer also goes nicely with these dishes.

SHOPPING LIST AND STAPLES

Eight 1-inch-thick, center-cut pork chops (about 1¾ pounds total weight), boned and pounded to ⅛-inch thickness

16 medium-size shrimp (¾ to 1 pound total weight)

1 large or 2 medium-size avocados

1¾ pounds fresh tomatoes, or 1 pound fresh plus 16-ounce can Italian plum tomatoes

1 head Bibb lettuce (optional)

2 medium-size onions

Small bunch scallions

Small bunch coriander

2 large mild fresh green chilies, or 4-ounce can

3 cloves garlic

1 lime

2 eggs

2 tablespoons unsalted butter

¼ pound Parmesan cheese

2 cups chicken stock, preferably homemade (see page 13) or canned

6 tablespoons vegetable oil, approximately

½ teaspoon white wine vinegar

Hot pepper sauce

¼ pound vermicelli

½ cup flour

¼ teaspoon dried oregano

Salt and freshly ground pepper

UTENSILS

Food processor or blender

Large skillet, preferably nonstick, with cover

Large saucepan

2 small saucepans

9-inch pie plate

Plate

Platter

Colander

Salad spinner (optional)

Sieve

Measuring cups and spoons

Chef's knife

Paring knife

Wooden spoon

Slotted metal spatula

Rubber spatula

Fork

Small paper bag

START-TO-FINISH STEPS

1. If using fresh tomatoes, bring 3 quarts water to a boil in large saucepan over high heat. Plunge tomatoes into boiling water and leave 30 seconds. Turn tomatoes into colander, refresh under cold running water, and drain. Remove peel. Core, halve, seed, and coarsely chop. If using canned tomatoes, drain.

2. Follow pork recipe steps 1 through 3.

3. While sauce is simmering, follow guacamole recipe steps 1 through 4.

4. Follow vermicelli recipe steps 1 through 4.

5. Follow pork recipe steps 4 through 10 and keep warm until ready to serve.

6. Follow vermicelli recipe steps 5 through 7.

7. While vermicelli is cooking, follow guacamole recipe steps 5 through 9 and serve.

8. Follow pork recipe step 11, vermicelli recipe step 8, and serve.

RECIPES

Shrimp Guacamole

1¼ teaspoons salt

16 medium-size shrimp (¾ to 1 pound total weight)

2 scallions

Medium-size clove garlic

Bibb lettuce leaves for garnish (optional)

¼ cup coriander leaves, loosely packed

2 teaspoons lime juice

Hot pepper sauce

Large tomato (about ½ pound)

1. Peel shrimp (see page 50), leaving 4 shrimp with tails attached, and devein. Rinse, drain, and pat dry.

2. In small saucepan, bring 3 cups water and ½ teaspoon salt to a boil over high heat.

3. Add shrimp and boil 2 minutes, or until they have turned pink and are barely firm.

4. Turn shrimp into colander and refresh under cold running water. Drain and set aside.

5. Wash, pat dry, and trim scallions, leaving about 3 inches of green. Peel garlic. Combine scallions and garlic in bowl of food processor or blender and chop.

6. Wash lettuce, if using, and coriander, and dry in salad spinner or pat dry with paper towels.

7. Cut avocado in half lengthwise, remove pit, and scoop flesh into processor.

8. Reserve the 4 shrimp with tails still attached for garnish. Add remaining shrimp, tomato, coriander, lime juice, remaining ¾ teaspoon salt, and hot pepper sauce to processor and process mixture just until blended but still somewhat chunky. Do not overprocess.

9. Line each of 4 salad plates with lettuce leaves and top with guacamole. Garnish each serving with one of the reserved shrimp.

Pork Cutlets with Tomato Sauce

Medium-size clove garlic
Medium-size onion
¾ pound fresh tomatoes, peeled, seeded, and chopped, or 16-ounce can Italian plum tomatoes, drained
1 teaspoon salt
¼ teaspoon dried oregano, crumbled
Freshly ground pepper
½ teaspoon white wine vinegar
2 eggs
½ cup flour
Eight 1-inch-thick, center-cut pork chops (about 1¾ pounds total weight), boned and pounded to ⅛-inch thickness
2 tablespoons unsalted butter
2 tablespoons vegetable oil

1. Peel garlic. Peel and halve onion.
2. Combine garlic, onion, and prepared tomatoes in bowl of food processor or blender, and purée.
3. Transfer tomato mixture to small saucepan. Add ½ teaspoon salt, oregano, pepper, and vinegar, and stir until blended. Bring to a boil over medium heat. Lower heat and simmer, uncovered, 30 minutes, or until sauce is reduced to 1 cup. Cover and set aside.
4. Break eggs into 9-inch pie plate and beat until combined.
5. In paper bag, combine flour, ½ teaspoon salt, and pepper; shake to blend. Add 4 cutlets to bag and shake to coat.
6. Preheat oven to 250 degrees.
7. In skillet used for vermicelli, heat butter and oil over medium heat.
8. Shake each cutlet gently to remove excess flour, dip in beaten egg to coat both sides, and place in skillet. Reserve

flour in bag. Cook cutlets about 4 minutes or until first side is golden and egg is set. Turn cutlets and cook another 4 minutes.

9. Just before cutlets are done, flour remaining 4 cutlets.
10. Transfer cooked cutlets to platter and place in warm oven until ready to serve. Repeat process for remaining cutlets.
11. When ready to serve, remove cutlets from oven, divide among dinner plates, and top each with tomato sauce.

Mexican-Style Vermicelli

2 large mild fresh green chilies, roasted, peeled, and seeded, or 2 canned, rinsed, and drained
Medium-size clove garlic
½ medium-size onion
¼ pound vermicelli
3 to 4 tablespoons vegetable oil
2 tomatoes (about ½ pound total weight), cored, halved, and seeded
2 cups chicken stock
½ teaspoon salt
¼ cup grated Parmesan cheese, approximately

1. Prepare chilies (see pages 9, 10) and chop.
2. Peel and mince garlic. Peel onion and finely chop.
3. Line a plate with paper towels.
4. Break vermicelli into small pieces. In large skillet, preferably nonstick, heat 3 tablespoons oil over medium heat. Add vermicelli and sauté gently, stirring frequently, 3 to 4 minutes, or until lightly browned. Transfer vermicelli with slotted metal spatula to paper-towel-lined plate.
5. To same skillet used for cutlets, add onion, garlic, and remaining tablespoon oil, if necessary. Add onion and garlic, and sauté over medium heat until tender, about 4 minutes.
6. Add tomatoes and chilies, and bring to a simmer over medium-high heat. Simmer, uncovered, 5 minutes.
7. Add chicken stock and salt, and stir until blended. Raise heat to high and bring to a boil. Stir in vermicelli and reduce heat to a simmer. Cover pan and simmer gently, stirring occasionally, until vermicelli is tender and all stock has been absorbed, 10 to 15 minutes. (If using a pasta thicker than vermicelli, cooking time may increase to 20 to 25 minutes.)
8. Divide vermicelli among 4 dinner plates and top with grated Parmesan cheese.

Rick Bayless

A linguist and anthropologist, as well as a cook, Rick Bayless is especially interested in Mexico and its diverse regional foods. He has discovered that each little Mexican town has its own unique recipes, and he goes directly to the street vendors and food stalls to watch and sample. His own recipes adapt this traditional Mexican fare for the American kitchen, using easily obtainable ingredients.

Menu 1, an informal meal for a fall or winter evening, starts with a chicken soup named for Tlalpán, a suburb of Mexico City. The main course, cheese *empanadas*, is a variation on Mexican turnovers, which are frequently filled with savory pork, chicken, or fish mixtures. Rather than using a conventional pastry, he has developed a quick biscuit-like dough of cornmeal and chili powder. He prepares the green bean salad the same way he would a Mexican cactus (*nopal*) salad, here substituting the beans for the hard-to-find cactus. For Menu 2, he offers a tortilla casserole, a popular Mexican breakfast dish that often contains shredded chicken or chorizo sausage. His version, however, calls for eggs and bacon. The pickled cauliflower, a recipe he learned from a Mexico City cook, is a variation on the pickled peppers often served at Mexican restaurants.

Yucatecan foods are the basis for Menu 3: black bean *tostadas* and chicken in *escabeche*, a spicy "pickling" sauce, both variations of traditional dishes of the southeastern peninsula.

Bowls of chili-spiced chicken soup, garnished with refreshing avocado slices, introduce this family-style meal. Serve the festive salad and the cheese-filled empanadas on separate dishes.

Chicken Soup Tlalpeño
Cheese Empanadas
Green Bean Salad

Salsas are staple condiments at the Mexican table. Whether hot or mild, they are tomato- or chili-based and have a relish-like consistency. The cook suggests serving a medium-hot salsa with the empanadas, but you can vary its piquancy to suit your tastes. Use a fresh salsa as soon as possible, preferably the same day you make it; it loses its flavor as it ages.

If you cannot find *chipotle* chilies, which give the chicken soup its smoky piquancy, use a pure chili powder instead (for information, see page 10). The avocado provides a cooling contrast to the fiery *chipotles*.

WHAT TO DRINK

A chilled, crisp white Muscadet from France or a young and fruity California Zinfandel would go well with this lively menu, but a good dark Mexican beer would be even better.

SHOPPING LIST AND STAPLES

2 chicken breasts, skinned and boned (about 1 pound total weight)
Small avocado
Medium-size ripe tomato (about ½ pound)
Small head Romaine lettuce
Small bunch radishes
Large carrot
Large onion (about ¾ pound)
Large clove garlic
Small bunch coriander
Small bunch parsley (optional)
Large lime (optional)
6 cups chicken stock, preferably homemade (see page 13) or canned
15-ounce can chick-peas (garbanzos)
4-ounce can whole chipotle chilies, or 1 teaspoon pure chili powder
4-ounce can diced mild green chilies
½ cup milk
¼ pound Monterey Jack cheese
¼ pound Mexican white cheese, farmer, or feta cheese
⅓ cup olive oil
1 tablespoon vegetable oil
⅓ cup vegetable shortening
2 tablespoons cider vinegar
1⅓ cups flour
2 tablespoons cornmeal

1 teaspoon sugar
1 teaspoon baking powder
1½ teaspoons New Mexico (hot), California (mild), or other pure chili powder
¾ teaspoon *fines herbes* (marjoram, thyme, etc.)
½ teaspoon dried oregano
Small bay leaf
Salt
Freshly ground black pepper

UTENSILS

Food processor (optional)
2 large saucepans, one with cover
11 × 17-inch baking sheet
Large bowl (if not using processor)
2 medium-size bowls
Small bowl
Small jar with tight-fitting lid
Colander
Measuring cups and spoons
Chef's knife
Paring knife
Wooden spoon
Slotted spoon
Ladle
Fork
Metal spatula
Grater (if not using processor)
Vegetable peeler (optional)

START-TO-FINISH STEPS

1. Peel and dice onion for soup and salad. Rinse and drain chilies for empanadas and for soup. Wash and pat dry coriander, Romaine, and parsley, if using. Chop coriander and parsley. Wrap lettuce in paper towels and refrigerate until ready to compose salad. Trim green beans.
2. Follow soup recipe steps 1 through 6.
3. While soup base is simmering, follow salad recipe step 1.
4. Follow empanadas recipe steps 1 through 3.
5. Follow salad recipe steps 2 through 5.
6. Follow empanadas recipe steps 4 through 7.
7. Follow soup recipe steps 7 and 8.
8. Follow salad recipe steps 6 and 7.
9. Follow empanadas recipe step 8, soup recipe steps 9 and 10, and serve with salad.

Chicken Soup Tlalpeño

15-ounce can chick-peas (garbanzos)
1 to 2 canned whole chipotle chilies, rinsed, drained, and
    seeded, or 1 teaspoon pure chili powder
½ cup diced carrot
1 tablespoon vegetable oil
1¼ cups diced onion
1 large clove garlic
6 cups chicken stock
¾ teaspoon *fines herbes* (marjoram, thyme, etc.)
Small bay leaf
2 chicken breasts, skinned and boned
Salt
Small avocado
Large lime for garnish (optional)

1. Rinse chick-peas under cold running water and drain.
2. Cut chilies, if using, into ¹⁄₁₆- to ¼-inch julienne.
3. Peel carrot and cut into ¼-inch dice.
4. In large saucepan, heat oil over medium heat. Add carrot and onion and cook, stirring occasionally, 5 minutes, or until onion is translucent.
5. Place garlic clove under flat of knife blade and lean down on blade with heel of your hand to crush garlic. Add garlic to pan and cook, stirring, another 2 minutes.
6. Stir in chick-peas, stock, and herbs. Raise heat to medium-high and bring soup to a simmer. Reduce heat to medium-low, partially cover saucepan, and simmer soup 30 to 40 minutes.
7. Cut chicken breast into ½-inch-wide strips and then cut strips into ½-inch dice.
8. With slotted spoon, remove garlic clove and bay leaf from soup; discard. Stir in diced chicken and chilies or chili powder. Simmer soup another 5 minutes, or just long enough to cook chicken through. Add salt to taste.
9. Peel, halve, and pit avocado. Cut each half lengthwise into 4 wedges. Quarter lime, if using.
10. Ladle soup into individual bowls and float 2 slices of avocado in each bowl. Serve with lime wedges, if desired.

Cheese Empanadas

1 cup grated Monterey Jack cheese
2 tablespoons canned diced mild green chilies, rinsed
    and drained
1⅓ cups flour, approximately
2 tablespoons cornmeal
1½ teaspoons New Mexico (hot), California (mild), or
    other pure chili powder
1 teaspoon baking powder
1 teaspoon sugar
¼ teaspoon salt
⅓ cup vegetable shortening
½ cup milk
1 tablespoon chopped parsley for garnish (optional)

1. Preheat oven to 400 degrees.
2. In food processor or with grater, grate cheese.

3. In medium-size bowl, combine cheese and chilies. Divide mixture into 4 portions and press each into a flat oval about 2½ inches long and 1 inch wide; set aside.
4. Blend 1 cup flour, cornmeal, chili powder, baking powder, sugar, salt, and vegetable shortening in food processor fitted with steel blade. With machine running, add milk in a steady stream and process until dough forms a ball. If not using processor, combine dry ingredients in large bowl. With fork or your fingers, work in shortening until blended. Add milk and work mixture until dough forms a ball. Dough will be sticky.
5. Generously flour work surface. Place dough on work surface and dust well with flour. Pat into a ¼-inch-thick square and cut into quarters, forming 4 small squares. Turn each square so that one point is facing toward you.
6. Place one of the reserved cheese ovals on right half of each of the 4 squares. Bring the left half of square over the right so points meet and filling is enclosed. Crimp edges.
7. Transfer empanadas to ungreased baking sheet and bake about 12 minutes, or until golden brown.
8. Transfer empanadas to platter and sprinkle with parsley, if desired.

Green Bean Salad

1 tablespoon plus ⅛ teaspoon salt
¾ pound fresh green beans, trimmed
1 medium-size ripe tomato (about ½ pound)
¼ cup diced onion
1 tablespoon chopped coriander
2 radishes, cut into ⅛-inch-thick slices
2 tablespoons cider vinegar
½ teaspoon dried oregano
Freshly ground black pepper
⅓ cup olive oil
Several leaves Romaine lettuce
3 tablespoons crumbled Mexican white cheese, farmer,
    or feta cheese

1. In large saucepan, bring 3 quarts water and 1 tablespoon salt to a boil, covered, over medium-high heat.
2. Add green beans to boiling water and cook, uncovered, 5 to 7 minutes, or just until beans are crisp tender.
3. While beans are cooking, add tomato to same pan and cook 30 seconds. With slotted spoon, transfer tomato to colander, refresh under cold running water, and remove peel. Halve, core, and seed tomato; cut into ½-inch dice and place in small bowl. Add onion and coriander, and toss to combine.
4. When beans are done, transfer them to colander, refresh under cold running water, drain, and allow to cool.
5. In small jar with lid, combine vinegar, oregano, ⅛ teaspoon salt, and pepper to taste. Cover jar and shake well to blend. Add olive oil and shake until blended.
6. Combine green beans and diced tomato in medium-size bowl. Toss with dressing until evenly coated.
7. Line a small, deep serving platter with Romaine lettuce leaves. Mound green bean salad in center and sprinkle with radish slices and crumbled cheese.

Tortilla Casserole
Pickled Cauliflower

Offer individual servings of the layered tortilla casserole—garnished with crumbled cheese, cream, parsley, and *radish slices—with a helping of cauliflower and carrots on the side.*

This tortilla casserole, also known as *chilaquiles*, is an ideal way to use up leftover tortillas. Quick-frying softens tortillas. Cook them for a few seconds on each side until limp but not crisp. If you use frozen tortillas that have been defrosted, spread them out for a few minutes in a single layer to dry; any moisture will cause spattering when you fry them.

You can vary the pickled cauliflower by adding any crisp, fresh vegetables you have on hand. The flavors of this dish improve if you make it a day ahead.

WHAT TO DRINK

Beer or ale, iced tea, or iced coffee are preferable to wine here because of the variety of sweet and sour flavors.

SHOPPING LIST AND STAPLES

8 slices bacon (about ½ pound)
Small head cauliflower (about 1½ pounds)
2 large carrots (about ½ pound total weight)
Large onion
9 large cloves garlic
4 fresh jalapeño or serrano chilies, or 4-ounce can, whole
Small bunch fresh parsley (optional)
8 eggs
½ pint heavy cream
½ pint sour cream
2 ounces Mexican white cheese, farmer, or feta cheese
12 fresh corn tortillas, or 1 package frozen
⅔ cup chicken stock, preferably homemade (see page 13), or canned
28-ounce can tomatoes, packed in juice
¾ cup vegetable oil
⅓ cup cider vinegar
1½ tablespoons New Mexico (hot), California (mild), or other pure chili powder
½ teaspoon dried marjoram
½ teaspoon dried thyme
2 bay leaves
Salt and freshly ground black pepper

UTENSILS

Food processor or blender
2 large skillets, one with cover
Small skillet
Medium-size saucepan

11 x 17-inch cookie sheet
8 x 8 x 2-inch baking dish
2 small bowls
Colander
Strainer
Measuring cups and spoons
Chef's knife
Paring knife
Wooden spoon
Tongs
Fork

START-TO-FINISH STEPS

One hour ahead: If using frozen tortillas for casserole, set out to thaw.

1. Peel onion and halve crosswise. Coarsely chop one half for casserole recipe and slice remaining half for cauliflower recipe. Peel garlic. Coarsely chop 5 cloves for casserole and halve 4 cloves lengthwise for cauliflower.
2. Follow casserole recipe steps 1 and 2.
3. Follow cauliflower recipe steps 1 through 4.
4. Follow casserole recipe steps 3 through 6.
5. Follow cauliflower recipe step 5.
6. Follow casserole recipe steps 7 through 13 and serve with cauliflower.

RECIPES

Tortilla Casserole

28-ounce can tomatoes, packed in juice
½ cup chopped onion
5 large cloves garlic
1½ tablespoons New Mexico (hot), California (mild), or other pure chili powder
⅔ cup chicken stock
Salt
8 slices of bacon (about ½ pound)
½ cup vegetable oil
12 fresh corn tortillas, or 1 package frozen
2 ounces Mexican white cheese, farmer, or feta cheese
8 eggs
Freshly ground black pepper
¾ cup sour cream
¼ cup heavy cream
1 tablespoon chopped fresh parsley for garnish (optional)

1. Drain tomatoes and place in food processor fitted with metal blade or in blender. Reserve juice for another purpose. Add onion, garlic, and chili powder to tomatoes and process until smooth.

2. Transfer mixture to medium-size saucepan. Add stock and ½ teaspoon salt and bring to a simmer over medium-high heat. Reduce heat to medium-low and simmer tomato sauce, uncovered, about 15 minutes.

3. Cut bacon into 1-inch pieces. In large skillet, cook bacon, stirring frequently, over medium heat until golden brown and crisp, about 5 minutes.

4. Preheat oven to 375 degrees and line cookie sheet with paper towels.

5. In small skillet, heat vegetable oil over medium-high heat. When oil is almost smoking, quickly fry tortillas, one at a time, about 3 seconds per side, or just until soft and pliable. With tongs, transfer tortillas as they are done to paper-towel-lined cookie sheet.

6. When bacon is done, remove skillet from heat and carefully drain off all but 1 tablespoon fat.

7. Crumble enough cheese to measure ½ cup; set aside.

8. Return skillet with bacon to heat and reduce to medium-low. Crack eggs into skillet, break yolks, and scramble eggs with bacon until eggs are firm but still soft. Stir in two thirds of the crumbled cheese and remove pan from heat. Sprinkle with salt and pepper to taste.

9. Line bottom of 8 x 8 x 2-inch baking dish with 4 tortillas, overlapping where necessary. Spread half of bacon and egg mixture over tortillas and top with one third of tomato sauce (about ¾ cup). Repeat with 4 more tortillas, remaining half of bacon and egg mixture, and half of remaining sauce. Top with remaining 4 tortillas and completely cover with tomato sauce.

10. Bake, uncovered, until heated through and bubbling around edges, about 10 minutes.

11. While casserole is baking, combine sour cream and heavy cream in small bowl and stir until blended.

12. If using parsley, wash and pat dry. Chop enough parsley to measure 1 tablespoon.

13. Remove baking dish from oven and top with remaining crumbled cheese. Sprinkle with chopped parsley, if desired. Cut into squares and divide among individual plates. Serve remaining cream sauce separately.

Pickled Cauliflower

4 fresh jalapeño or serrano chilies, or 4 canned, rinsed, drained, and patted dry
1½ cups sliced carrots
¼ cup vegetable oil
4 large cloves garlic
½ cup sliced onion
Small head cauliflower (about 1½ pounds)
⅓ cup cider vinegar
½ teaspoon dried marjoram
½ teaspoon thyme
¾ teaspoon salt
¼ teaspoon freshly ground black pepper
2 bay leaves

1. If using fresh chilies, wash and pat dry. If using canned, prepare and set aside. Peel carrots and cut into ¼-inch-thick slices.

2. Heat oil in large, deep skillet over medium heat. Add sliced garlic, onion, carrots, and fresh chilies, if using. Toss to combine and cook, stirring frequently, about 5 minutes, until onion is soft.

3. Peel leaves from cauliflower. Turn cauliflower stem end up and, with sharp paring knife, remove core. Break head into large pieces and cut pieces in large florets. Place florets in colander and wash thoroughly under cold running water; drain.

4. In small bowl, combine vinegar, ¼ cup water, marjoram, thyme, salt, and pepper. Stir until blended and add to sautéed vegetables along with bay leaves. Add cauliflower, toss to combine, cover, and cook 8 to 10 minutes, or until cauliflower is just tender.

5. If using canned chilies, add to vegetables and adjust seasoning if necessary. Turn vegetables and cooking liquid out onto serving platter and let cool to room temperature, basting frequently with cooking liquid as they cool.

___

ADDED TOUCH

The easiest way to form these fritters (*churros*) is to use a cookie press. They are most delicious served hot.

Cinnamon Fritter Sticks

2 tablespoons vegetable oil
1 tablespoon sugar
½ teaspoon cinnamon
2 teaspoons salt
1 cup flour
Oil for deep frying
⅔ cup cinnamon sugar

1. In medium-size saucepan, bring oil, 1 cup water, sugar, cinnamon, and salt to a boil.

2. As soon as mixture boils, remove pan from heat and add flour, beating vigorously until smooth. Batter will be very thick and form a smooth-textured ball. Let dough cool until it can be handled.

3. Fill medium-size skillet ½-inch full of oil and heat over medium-high heat until oil registers 375 degrees on deep-fat thermometer. (Measure temperature by very carefully tilting skillet to one side.)

4. Line a platter with paper towels.

5. Spoon batter into cookie press or pastry bag fitted with ⅜-inch fluted tip. Pipe out several 5-inch lengths at a time and drop into hot oil at least an inch apart. Cook 3 to 4 minutes, turning to brown evenly.

6. When browned, transfer fritters with tongs or slotted spoon to paper-towel-lined platter. Taste one. If it is doughy inside, let oil cool slightly and then return fritters to pan and fry another minute. Repeat process until batter is used up, increasing cooking time if necessary.

7. In brown paper bag, dredge warm fritters with cinnamon sugar. Serve immediately.

Black Bean Tostadas
Chicken in Escabeche

Pieces of chicken in escabeche, *served in an earthenware bowl, are garnished with sprigs of coriander and red onion slices. Arrange the tostadas, layered with black beans, cream, and vegetable garnishes, on a platter.*

Chicken pieces crowded into a skillet will steam rather than brown, so be sure to use a skillet roomy enough for these chicken quarters, or brown them in two medium-size skillets and then consolidate them. If you have time, prepare the chicken in *escabeche* a day ahead to allow the flavor to develop; reheat before serving. Served cold, this dish is also ideal for picnics.

Tostadas are open-face "sandwiches" on a crisp fried tortilla base. The black beans for the filling are sold in cans in most supermarkets or specialty food shops. You can use dried beans instead (see page 11), but you must start the recipe the night before. Soak one half pound of dried beans overnight, then drain them the next morning. Cover them with fresh water and simmer them about two hours, or until tender. Pinto or kidney beans are acceptable substitutes, but are not typical of Yucatecan cooking.

To fry crisp, the corn tortillas must be thin and thoroughly dry. The oil should be hot (375 degrees, or hot enough to brown a bread cube within 60 seconds) but *not* smoking.

WHAT TO DRINK

A firm, dry white wine would be a sprightly partner for this flavorful menu. Try a good Mâcon or St. Véran from Burgundy or a California Chardonnay.

SHOPPING LIST AND STAPLES

1 large chicken (about 3½ pounds), quartered
Small head Romaine lettuce
Small bunch radishes
Medium-size yellow onion
Large red onion
5 large cloves garlic
Small bunch coriander
Two 16-ounce cans black, pinto, or kidney beans
½ pint sour cream
½ pint heavy cream
¼ pound Mexican white cheese, farmer, or feta cheese
8 fresh corn tortillas, or 1 package frozen
⅔ cup vegetable oil, approximately
¼ cup olive oil
2 tablespoons bacon drippings, preferably, or lard or vegetable oil
⅔ cup cider vinegar
½ cup flour

½ teaspoon oregano
½ teaspoon ground allspice
¼ teaspoon thyme
¼ teaspoon marjoram
¼ teaspoon ground cloves
4 bay leaves
Salt
Freshly ground black pepper

UTENSILS

2 large skillets with covers
Small skillet
11 × 17-inch cookie sheet
Heatproof serving platter
Medium-size nonaluminum bowl
2 small bowls
Colander
Salad spinner (optional)
Measuring cups and spoons
Chef's knife
Paring knife
Wooden spoon
Potato masher (optional)
Tongs
Deep-fat thermometer (optional)
Brown paper bag

START-TO-FINISH STEPS

One hour ahead: If using frozen tortillas for tostadas, set out to thaw.

1. Peel and mince garlic for tostadas and chicken recipes. Peel onions, dice yellow onion for tostadas recipe; slice red onion for chicken recipe. Set aside.
2. Follow tostadas recipe steps 1 through 4.
3. Follow chicken recipe steps 1 and 2.
4. Follow tostadas recipe steps 5 and 6.
5. While beans are cooking, follow chicken recipe steps 3 through 5.
6. Check beans. If done, replace cover, remove pan from heat, and while chicken is cooking, follow tostadas recipe steps 7 and 8.
7. Follow chicken recipe steps 6 through 8.
8. While chicken continues cooking, follow tostadas recipe step 9.
9. Follow chicken recipe steps 9 through 11, and serve with tostadas.

RECIPES

Black Bean Tostadas

⅔ cup vegetable oil, approximately
8 fresh corn tortillas, or 8 frozen tortillas, thawed
2 tablespoons bacon drippings, preferably, or lard or vegetable oil
1¼ cups diced yellow onion

Two 16-ounce cans black, pinto, or kidney beans
1 tablespoon minced garlic
½ teaspoon salt, approximately
8 leaves Romaine lettuce
3 radishes
½ cup sour cream
3 tablespoons heavy cream
½ cup crumbled Mexican white cheese, farmer, or feta cheese

1. Line cookie sheet with paper towels.
2. Heat ⅓ cup vegetable oil in small skillet over medium-high heat. When oil reaches 375 degrees, add a tortilla and fry about 30 seconds. With tongs, turn tortilla and fry another 30 seconds, or until crisp. Transfer tortilla to cookie sheet. Repeat with remaining tortillas until all are fried, adding more oil and adjusting temperature as needed.
3. In large skillet, heat bacon drippings over medium heat. Add onion and cook, stirring frequently, 5 to 6 minutes, or until soft.
4. In colander, rinse beans gently under cold running water and drain.
5. Add garlic to onions and cook, stirring, another 2 minutes.
6. Add beans and, using back of wooden spoon or potato masher, mash into coarse purée, adding up to ¼ cup water if beans seem dry. Add salt to taste. Cover skillet, reduce heat to low, and cook 5 to 10 minutes, until beans are heated through.
7. Wash Romaine leaves and dry in salad spinner or pat dry with paper towels. Wash, pat dry, and trim radishes. Stack lettuce leaves end to end and cut into ¼- to ½-inch-wide strips. Cut radishes crosswise into ¼-inch-thick slices.
8. In small bowl, combine sour cream with heavy cream.
9. To assemble tostadas, carefully spread each tortilla with about 3 tablespoons beans. Top each with a dollop of cream mixture, equal portions of shredded lettuce and radish slices, and 1 tablespoon crumbled cheese.

Chicken in Escabeche

1½ cups thinly sliced red onion, approximately
2 teaspoons minced garlic
⅔ cup cider vinegar
½ teaspoon oregano, plus additional ½ teaspoon
½ teaspoon ground allspice, plus additional ¼ teaspoon
4 bay leaves
½ cup flour
1 large chicken (about 3½ pounds), quartered
¼ cup olive oil
¾ teaspoon salt
½ teaspoon freshly ground black pepper
¼ teaspoon thyme
¼ teaspoon marjoram
¼ teaspoon ground cloves
Coriander sprigs for garnish

1. Separate onion into rings and combine with garlic in nonaluminum bowl. Add vinegar, ½ cup water, ½ teaspoon oregano, ½ teaspoon allspice, and bay leaves. Stir to combine and set aside.

2. Preheat oven to 200 degrees.

3. Place flour in brown paper bag. Add chicken quarters, 2 at a time, and shake until coated. Remove chicken from bag and set aside.

4. In large skillet, heat olive oil over medium heat.

5. When oil is hot, add dark-meat quarters of chicken skin-side down and fry 8 minutes, or until golden.

6. Turn chicken and add white-meat quarters skin-side down. Fry 4 minutes.

7. Combine salt, pepper, thyme, marjoram, cloves, and remaining oregano and allspice in small bowl.

8. Turn white-meat quarters and, reserving onion, add vinegar-spice marinade from the onion to skillet. Sprinkle with herb-and-spice mixture, reduce heat to medium-low, partially cover, and simmer about 12 minutes, or until chicken is tender.

9. Transfer chicken to heatproof platter and place in oven to keep warm. Add reserved onions to skillet, increase heat to medium-high, and cook 2 to 3 minutes, just to eliminate raw taste but not crunchiness.

10. Wash coriander sprigs and pat dry.

11. To serve, pour onion and cooking liquid over chicken and garnish with coriander sprigs.

ADDED TOUCH

This old-fashioned dessert, often served in Mexico with assorted exotic fruits, is flavored with Jamaican rum.

Floating Island

1⅓ cups plus 1 tablespoon sugar
1 teaspoon freshly squeezed lemon juice
6 eggs, at room temperature, separated
⅛ teaspoon salt
Pinch of cream of tartar
1 teaspoon vanilla extract
1½ cups milk
1½ tablespoons dark Jamaican rum
1 large, ripe mango
1 pint strawberries

1. Lightly grease an 11 × 17-inch baking sheet.

2. Place ½ cup sugar in small heavy-gauge nonaluminum saucepan. Sprinkle sugar with lemon juice and 3 tablespoons water. Do not stir. Bring mixture to a boil over high heat.

3. When mixture has come to a boil, swirl pan carefully to dissolve sugar and brush down sides of pan with pastry brush dipped in cold water.

4. Let mixture boil undisturbed about 3 to 5 minutes, or until it turns a light amber color.

5. Swirl pan to distribute color, and immediately pour mixture onto greased baking sheet, and let cool. (Caramelized sugar will harden as it cools.) Rinse and dry pan.

6. When cool, pry sugar away from baking sheet, break

into small pieces, and pulverize in blender or food processor until powdery. Scrape into small bowl.

7. Preheat oven to 250 degrees.

8. Butter a 1½- to 2-quart straight-sided soufflé or baking dish. Place a tablespoon of sugar in dish and rotate dish, tilting it to coat sides; set aside.

9. Bring 2 quarts of water to a boil in medium-size nonaluminum saucepan.

10. For meringue, beat egg whites with electric mixer at medium speed until foamy. Add salt and cream of tartar, and continue to beat until whites hold stiff peaks.

11. Add ½ cup sugar, 1 tablespoon at a time, beating 30 seconds after each addition. Continue to beat meringue 3 to 4 minutes, or until very stiff, glossy, and smooth. Beat in ½ teaspoon vanilla and 2 tablespoons of the powdered caramelized sugar. Turn mixture into prepared soufflé or baking dish.

12. Place soufflé dish in another slightly larger oven-proof dish. Pour the boiling water into larger dish until water reaches a depth of 2 inches. Empty remaining water from saucepan and dry.

13. Bake meringue 40 to 50 minutes, or until light brown and firm and a toothpick inserted in center comes out clean.

14. Meanwhile, for custard sauce, heat milk in nonaluminum saucepan used for sugar until it steams.

15. With electric mixer at high speed, beat egg yolks and remaining ⅓ cup sugar in large bowl 3 to 4 minutes, until thick and lemon-colored. Add steaming hot milk and 2 tablespoons powdered caramelized sugar, beating steadily until incorporated.

16. Return egg-milk mixture to the medium-size nonaluminum saucepan and cook, stirring, over medium-low heat until mixture thickens slightly and coats back of wooden spoon. Do not permit mixture to boil. Rinse and dry the large bowl.

17. Using a fine mesh sieve, strain custard back into the large bowl and stir in rum and remaining ½ teaspoon vanilla extract. Let cool to room temperature.

18. Meanwhile, when done, remove meringue from oven and let cool in its water bath.

19. Just before serving, peel mango and cut flesh away from pit in chunks. Place in small serving bowl.

20. In colander, rinse strawberries under cold, running water, drain, and gently pat dry. Reserve 8 whole berries for garnish. Hull and slice remainder and place in another small serving bowl.

21. Place a deep, wide serving platter over soufflé dish containing cooled meringue mixture. Holding the 2 dishes firmly together, invert, so that meringue unmolds onto center of platter.

22. Pour cooled custard around outside of meringue "island," stirring in any caramel liquid that may have extruded from the meringue.

23. Garnish platter with the reserved whole strawberries and sprinkle top of meringue with remaining powdered caramelized sugar. Serve slices of meringue with custard sauce spooned over top. Pass fruit separately.

Constantine Coules

Constantine Coules likes to prepare meals that emphasize the natural flavors and textures of food; thus he enjoys Mexican cooking, which combines fresh ingredients in particularly creative and colorful ways. The three menus here, although diverse, have bright colors in common. The main course of Menu 1 features crisp shrimp, rice, and kidney beans, surrounded by shredded Romaine lettuce. Black, red, brown, and yellow are the colors of Menu 2: black beans; red, slivered peppers; browned slices of beef; and yellow rice. In Menu 3, the brilliant carrot-pepper-pea sauté sets off the sea bass fillets.

When he cooks, Constantine Coules borrows heavily from many cuisines, mixing and matching ingredients and techniques. Sometimes the results are unexpected. For instance, Menu 1 starts with *gazpacho*, a Spanish soup of puréed raw vegetables, usually served cold but here served hot with a melted-cheese topping. For the main dish of Menu 2, he calls for beef, thinly sliced as the Japanese would for *sukiyaki*. Indian curry powder seasons the egg batter for the shrimp in Menu 1 and the rice in Menu 2, and red wine vinegar, a Spanish touch, is added to the white bean soup in Menu 3. (Menus 2 and 3 have no dairy products.)

For visual appeal, create concentric rings with the shredded lettuce, rice and beans, and shrimp. Garnish the hot gazpacho with chopped parsley and serve the sauce for the shrimp in a separate bowl.

Hot Gazpacho with Melted Cheese
Shrimp with Coriander-Citrus Sauce
Rice and Beans

Of the two varieties of Monterey Jack, the Editors suggest you use the semisoft, mild one made from whole milk, which melts more easily. As a substitute, try a Mexican *queso fresco* (see page 12) or Muenster. For serving the soup, you will need four ovenproof soup bowls or one large ovenproof serving bowl. (If you use the larger bowl, ladle the soup into warmed individual bowls.)

For the broiled shrimp, you might be able to buy raw shrimp with their shells and veins removed. If not, peel the shrimp, make a shallow cut along the curved backs, and carefully lift out the black vein with the tip of a paring knife or your fingers (see page 50).

Before broiling, dunk each shrimp in the beaten egg, then roll it in bread crumbs. For best results and to achieve the greatest volume, bring the egg to room temperature before beating it. As the shrimp broil, the egg-crumb coating should puff and brown.

WHAT TO DRINK

The cook suggests a moderately fruity, medium-bodied dry white wine, such as a white Rioja, to accompany this menu.

SHOPPING LIST AND STAPLES

2 dozen medium-size shrimp, shelled and deveined
    (about 1½ pounds total weight)
Small head Romaine lettuce
Small bunch celery
Large ripe tomato
Small green bell pepper
1 fresh serrano chili, or 1½ teaspoons hot pepper
    sauce
Medium-size Spanish onion
Medium-size clove garlic
Small bunch scallions
Small bunch coriander
Small bunch parsley
3 oranges
2 limes
1 egg
2 sticks plus 2 tablespoons butter,
    approximately
¼ pound Monterey Jack cheese
1¾ cups chicken stock, preferably homemade
    (see page 13), or canned

16-ounce can red kidney or pinto beans
12-ounce can tomato juice
1½ teaspoons hot pepper sauce, plus 1½ teaspoons
    (if not using fresh serrano chili)
⅓ cup olive oil, approximately, plus 3 tablespoons
3 teaspoons honey
1 cup long-grain white rice
1 cup fine, dry bread crumbs
Bay leaf
½ teaspoon curry powder
Salt
Freshly ground pepper

UTENSILS

Medium-size skillet
2 medium-size saucepans with covers
Small saucepan
Medium-size roasting pan
2 platters
4 ovenproof soup bowls, or 1 ovenproof serving bowl
2 small bowls
Colander
Salad spinner (optional)
Measuring cups and spoons
Chef's knife
Paring knife
Slotted spoon or metal wok spatula
Ladle
Grater
Juicer (optional)

START-TO-FINISH STEPS

1. Wash parsley and coriander for gazpacho and shrimp recipes. Pat dry and chop. Wash lettuce for shrimp and dry in salad spinner or pat dry with paper towels. Coarsely shred enough to measure 3 cups. Wrap in paper towels and refrigerate.
2. Follow gazpacho recipe steps 1 through 3.
3. While soup is simmering, follow rice and beans recipe steps 1 and 2.
4. While soup and rice are simmering, follow shrimp recipe step 1.
5. Follow rice and beans recipe steps 3 and 4.
6. Follow shrimp recipe steps 2 through 8.
7. Follow gazpacho recipe steps 4 and 5.

8. Follow shrimp recipe step 9.

9. Follow rice and beans recipe steps 5 and 6.

10. Follow shrimp recipe step 10 and serve with rice and beans and gazpacho.

RECIPES

Hot Gazpacho with Melted Cheese

Large tomato
1 fresh serrano chili, or 1½ teaspoons hot pepper sauce
1 stalk celery
Medium-size Spanish onion
Small green bell pepper
3 tablespoons chopped parsley
1¾ cups chicken stock
1½ cups tomato juice
Bay leaf
Salt
Freshly ground pepper
2 ounces Monterey Jack cheese

1. Bring 3 cups water to a boil in small saucepan over high heat. Blanch tomato 30 seconds. With slotted spoon, transfer to colander, refresh under cold running water, and drain. Peel, halve, seed, and dice.

2. If using fresh serrano chili, wash and pat dry. Seed, if desired, and dice. Wash celery; pat dry, trim, and chop. Peel onion and chop. Wash bell pepper and pat dry; core, halve, seed, and chop.

3. In medium-size saucepan, combine tomato, chili (if using), celery, onion, pepper, parsley, chicken stock, tomato juice, bay leaf, hot pepper sauce (if not using chili), and salt and freshly ground pepper to taste, and bring to a simmer over medium-high heat. Cover, reduce heat to low, and cook 25 minutes. Uncover and cook an additional 15 to 20 minutes.

4. Preheat oven to 500 degrees.

5. Ladle soup into individual ovenproof soup bowls or into large ovenproof serving bowl. Grate cheese and sprinkle individual bowls with 2 tablespoons each or large bowl with ½ cup. Bake in upper portion of oven 5 minutes, or until cheese has melted. Turn off oven. Hold soup in oven until serving time.

Shrimp with Coriander-Citrus Sauce

3 oranges
2 limes
½ teaspoon curry powder
1½ teaspoons hot pepper sauce
1 egg
1 cup fine, dry bread crumbs
2 dozen medium-size shrimp, shelled and deveined
   (about 1½ pounds total weight)
⅓ cup olive oil, approximately
2 sticks plus 2 tablespoons butter, approximately
3 teaspoons honey
3 tablespoons chopped coriander
Salt

3 cups coarsely shredded Romaine lettuce
Rice and Beans (see following recipe)

1. Grate enough orange rind to measure ½ cup. Squeeze enough oranges to measure ¾ cup juice and limes to measure 3 tablespoons juice; set aside.

2. Preheat broiler. Grease medium-size roasting pan with olive oil or butter.

3. In small bowl, beat curry powder and 1 teaspoon hot pepper sauce until blended. Add egg and beat thoroughly. Place bread crumbs in separate small bowl.

4. Dip shrimp first in egg mixture, then in bread crumbs, coating each shrimp evenly. Arrange in single layer in greased roasting pan, leaving space between them.

5. Drizzle breaded shrimp with 2 tablespoons olive oil and dot with 6 tablespoons butter.

6. Broil shrimp, turning once, about 7 minutes, or until cooked through and golden.

7. While shrimp are broiling, heat platter under running water. Drain and dry.

8. Transfer shrimp to warm platter and cover loosely with foil to keep warm.

9. Place roasting pan on range top over low heat. Add orange and lime juices, orange rind, honey, remaining ½ teaspoon hot pepper sauce, coriander, and salt to taste. Stir, scraping bottom of pan to incorporate drippings into sauce. Add remaining olive oil and butter to taste.

10. Arrange shrimp in center of platter and surround with concentric rings of shredded lettuce and Rice and Beans. Serve sauce separately.

Rice and Beans

3 tablespoons olive oil
1 cup long-grain white rice
1 teaspoon salt
16-ounce can red kidney or pinto beans
Medium-size clove garlic
3 to 4 scallions

1. Bring 2 cups water to a boil in small saucepan over medium-high heat.

2. Meanwhile, heat 2 tablespoons olive oil 10 to 15 seconds in medium-size saucepan over medium-high heat. Add rice and sauté, stirring, about 1 minute. Stir in boiling water and salt. Cover, reduce heat, and simmer 20 minutes, or until all liquid has been absorbed. Set aside and keep warm.

3. In colander, rinse and drain beans. Line platter with paper towels and turn beans onto platter. Blot dry with additional paper towels.

4. Peel and crush garlic clove. Trim scallions; wash, pat dry, and chop. Set aside.

5. Heat remaining tablespoon olive oil in medium-size skillet. Add garlic and scallions, and sauté, stirring, 10 to 15 seconds. Add beans and sauté, gently turning and stirring, 3 minutes, or until beans are heated through.

6. Fluff rice lightly with fork and turn into serving bowl. Add beans and toss gently to combine.

Beef in Spicy Tomato Sauce with Black Beans
Yellow Rice
Mango Salad

This nondairy meal features a main course of sautéed steak slices combined with red pepper strips and black beans, served on spicy rice. A light salad of sliced mangos and scallions is served on the side.

C umin, an assertive and aromatic spice commonly found in Indian and Mexican recipes, appears twice in this menu. As with all dried spices, cumin has the best flavor when it is freshly ground. If you like, buy whole cumin seeds and roast them lightly in an ungreased, heavy-gauge skillet over medium heat, a quarter of a cup at a time, stirring the seeds constantly to prevent scorching. When they have turned a pale chocolate color, remove the seeds from the skillet and grind them with a mortar and pestle.

WHAT TO DRINK

Try a fresh and fruity red wine with this hearty menu: a young California Gamay Beaujolais or Zinfandel.

SHOPPING LIST AND STAPLES

2 pounds boneless sirloin steak, cut in ⅛-inch-wide slices
Small head Bibb lettuce
Large red bell pepper
Large Spanish onion
2 cloves garlic
Small bunch scallions
Small bunch parsley
Small bunch coriander
2 medium-size mangos (1½ to 2 pounds total weight)
2 to 4 limes
16-ounce can black beans
6-ounce can tomato paste
¾ cup plus 2 tablespoons olive oil
1 teaspoon hot pepper sauce
1 cup long-grain white rice
1½ to 2 tablespoons ground cumin
1 tablespoon curry powder
Salt

UTENSILS

Large skillet
Medium-size skillet
2 medium-size saucepans, one preferably stainless steel or enamel and one with cover
Small saucepan
Platter
Small bowl
Colander
Salad spinner (optional)

Measuring cups and spoons
Chef's knife
Paring knife
Wooden spoon
Fork
Juicer (optional)
Garlic press

START-TO-FINISH STEPS

1. Wash coriander and parsley for beef and rice recipes; pat dry and chop. Trim scallions for rice and salad recipes; wash, pat dry, and chop.
2. Follow beef recipe steps 1 through 3.
3. While sauce simmers, follow rice recipe steps 1 through 3.
4. While sauce and rice are simmering, follow salad recipe steps 1 through 3.
5. Follow beef recipe steps 4 and 5, and remove rice from heat.
6. Follow beef recipe steps 6 through 9, rice recipe step 4, and salad recipe step 4.
7. Follow beef recipe step 10 and serve with rice and salad.

RECIPES

Beef in Spicy Tomato Sauce with Black Beans

Large Spanish onion
Large red bell pepper
2 cloves garlic
4 tablespoons olive oil
6-ounce can tomato paste
1½ to 2 tablespoons ground cumin
1 tablespoon chopped fresh coriander
1 teaspoon hot pepper sauce
16-ounce can black beans
Salt
2 pounds boneless sirloin steak, cut into ⅛-inch-wide slices
Yellow Rice (see following recipe)

1. Peel onion and cut into ¼-inch-thick slices; stack slices and cut in half crosswise. Wash pepper and pat dry. Core, halve, seed, and cut into julienne strips. Peel garlic and put through garlic press.
2. Heat 1 tablespoon olive oil in medium-size stainless steel or enamel saucepan over medium heat. Add onion, pepper, and garlic, and sauté, stirring, about 1 minute.
3. Stir in tomato paste, cumin, coriander, and hot pepper sauce, and cook, stirring, 1 to 2 minutes. Stir in 2 cups water, reduce heat to low, and cook, uncovered, about 45 minutes, stirring occasionally.
4. In colander, rinse beans under cold running water and drain. Transfer to paper-towel-lined platter; blot dry with additional paper towels.
5. In medium-size skillet, heat 1 tablespoon olive oil over medium heat about 10 seconds. Add beans and sauté gently, turning and stirring, about 3 minutes, or until heated through. Dry platter. Remove pan from heat and set aside.

6. Heat remaining 2 tablespoons olive oil in large skillet until oil begins to shimmer. Add beef slices and sauté very quickly, just until very rare. (Beef will continue to cook when sauce is added to it.) Transfer to platter.
7. Reduce beef liquid over medium-high heat, stirring constantly, until thickened. (If any juices have collected in platter holding meat, add them to skillet during reduction.)
8. While beef liquid is reducing, check sauce. If too thin, reduce over high heat, stirring constantly, 2 to 3 minutes; if too thin, add a tablespoon or more water. Add salt to taste.
9. Reduce heat under beef liquid to medium, return beef slices to skillet, and add warm sauce. Toss quickly to combine. Add beans and toss again.
10. Serve beef and bean mixture over Yellow Rice.

Yellow Rice

2 tablespoons olive oil
1 cup long-grain white rice
1 tablespoon curry powder
1 teaspoon salt
¼ cup chopped scallions
¼ cup chopped parsley

1. Bring 2 cups water to a boil in small saucepan over medium-high heat.
2. Meanwhile, heat 2 tablespoons olive oil 10 to 15 seconds in medium-size skillet over medium-high heat. Add rice and sauté, stirring, 30 seconds. Stir in curry powder and salt, and sauté rice another 30 seconds.
3. Stir in the boiling water, reduce heat to low, and cook, covered, about 20 minutes, or until water is completely absorbed.
4. Remove cover and fluff rice with fork. Add scallions and parsley, toss gently to combine, and turn into serving bowl.

Mango Salad

Small head Bibb lettuce
2 medium-size mangos (1½ to 2 pounds total weight)
2 to 4 limes
½ teaspoon salt
½ cup olive oil
2 tablespoons chopped scallions

1. Wash lettuce and dry in salad spinner or pat dry with paper towels. Line 4 individual bowls with lettuce, cover with plastic wrap, and refrigerate.
2. Peel mangos, slice flesh away from pit, as nearly in quarters as possible. Cover with plastic wrap and refrigerate.
3. Juice enough limes to measure ¼ cup. In small bowl, combine lime juice, salt, and olive oil, and beat until blended. Cover with plastic wrap.
4. Just before serving, divide mango slices among lettuce-lined bowls. Beat dressing to recombine and spoon over salads. Top with chopped scallions.

White Bean Soup
Yucatecan Sea Bass with Onions
Mixed Vegetable Sauté

Dark dinner plates highlight the colorful sautéed vegetables and lightly browned sea bass. White bean soup begins the meal.

Navy beans, also known as Yankee or pea beans, are the principle ingredient of the flavorful first-course soup. These are small white beans that hold their shape well when they are cooked. If you wish to use dried rather than canned beans, follow the instructions on page 11 for reconstituting beans.

For the fried fish, use fillets of sea bass or any other firm-textured fish such as red snapper. Be sure that the fillets are uniformly thin, or they will not cook through quickly and evenly.

WHAT TO DRINK

The cook suggests a full-bodied and flavorful white wine, such as a California Chardonnay or a French Mâcon.

SHOPPING LIST AND STAPLES

4 fillets of sea bass or any firm-textured white fish, ½ to ¾ inch thick (about 1⅓ pounds total weight)

2 pounds fresh peas, unshelled, or 10-ounce package frozen
Medium-size bunch carrots
Medium-size red bell pepper
2 large Spanish onions (about 1¼ pounds total weight)
3 to 4 cloves garlic
Small bunch parsley
Small bunch coriander
1 to 2 limes
1½ cups chicken stock, preferably homemade (see page 13), or canned
20-ounce can white beans
6-ounce can pitted black olives
1¼ cups olive oil
2 tablespoons red wine vinegar
¾ teaspoon hot pepper sauce
1 cup all-purpose white flour
Bay leaf
2 to 3 teaspoons ground cumin

Salt and freshly ground pepper
½ cup sweet sherry

UTENSILS

Large skillet
Medium-size skillet
2 medium-size saucepans
Medium-size ovenproof bowl
9-inch pie plate
2 plates
Colander
Measuring cups and spoons
Chef's knife
Paring knife
Wooden spoon
Ladle
Fork
Vegetable peeler (optional)
Grater
Juicer (optional)

START-TO-FINISH STEPS

1. Follow soup recipe step 1.
2. While soup is simmering, follow vegetables recipe steps 1 and 2, and fish recipe steps 1 through 3.
3. Follow vegetables recipe steps 3 and 4, and fish recipe steps 4 through 8.
4. Follow soup recipe step 2 and serve.
5. Follow fish recipe step 9 and serve with vegetables.

RECIPES

White Bean Soup

2 tablespoons olive oil
⅔ cup finely chopped Spanish onion
½ cup chopped celery
1½ cups chicken stock
20-ounce can white beans
1 clove garlic, crushed
2 tablespoons red wine vinegar
Salt and freshly ground pepper
½ cup sliced pitted black olives for garnish

1. Heat olive oil in medium-size saucepan over medium heat. Add onion and celery, and sauté, stirring, about 30 seconds. Add stock, 1½ cups water, white beans and their liquid, and garlic. Reduce heat and simmer, uncovered, about 45 minutes.
3. Just before serving, stir in 2 tablespoons wine vinegar and salt and pepper to taste. Divide soup among individual serving bowls and serve garnished with sliced olives.

Yucatecan Sea Bass with Onions

Large Spanish onion, cut into ¼-inch-thick slices
1 cup olive oil
1 to 2 cloves garlic, crushed

½ cup sweet sherry
Bay leaf
4 fillets of sea bass or any firm-textured white fish, ½ to ¾ inch thick (about 1⅓ pounds total weight)
1 cup all-purpose white flour
Salt and freshly ground pepper
2 tablespoons freshly squeezed lime juice

1. Separate sliced onion into rings.
2. Heat 1 tablespoon oil in large skillet over medium heat. Add onion and garlic, and sauté, stirring frequently, about 5 minutes, or until onion is translucent.
3. Reduce heat to low. Add sherry and bay leaf and continue to cook, uncovered, about 20 minutes, or until onion is tender and sherry is absorbed.
4. Wipe fish fillets with damp paper towels. Dredge fillets in flour and sprinkle with salt and pepper to taste.
5. With slotted spoon, transfer onions to plate; set aside.
6. Heat remaining olive oil in same skillet over medium-high heat. When oil shimmers, add fillets and cook about 2 minutes per side, or until fish flakes easily with fork.
7. Remove fillets from skillet, drain briefly on paper towels, and divide among dinner plates. Remove skillet from heat and pour off all but 2 tablespoons of the oil. Return to medium-high heat and, quickly, add reserved onion and lime juice. Cook 1 to 2 minutes, or just long enough to reheat onion, stirring constantly to prevent burning. Season with salt and pepper to taste.
8. Spoon onion over fish and keep warm in oven.
9. Remove fish from oven and serve.

Mixed Vegetable Sauté

2 pounds fresh peas, or 10-ounce package frozen
Salt
Medium-size red bell pepper, diced
2 cups shredded carrots
2 tablespoons olive oil
1 clove garlic, minced
2 to 3 teaspoons ground cumin
¾ teaspoon hot pepper sauce
Freshly ground pepper
1 tablespoon chopped fresh coriander

1. If using fresh peas, shell enough to measure 2 cups, rinse, and drain. Bring about 1½ quarts water and 1½ teaspoons salt to a boil in medium-size saucepan over high heat. Line plate with paper towels. Blanch peas a few seconds only. Drain in colander and refresh under cold running water. Transfer to paper-towel-lined plate; blot dry with additional paper towels. If using frozen peas, do not thaw or blanch; use straight from the package.
2. Preheat oven to 250 degrees.
3. Heat olive oil in medium-size skillet over high heat. Add peas, pepper, carrots, garlic, and cumin, and sauté, stirring constantly, about 5 minutes, or until vegetables are just tender. Remove from heat, add hot pepper sauce, salt and pepper to taste, and coriander.
4. Turn into ovenproof bowl and keep warm in oven.

Vickie Simms

Vickie Simms cooks California-style Mexican food, mixing Mexican spices and other seasonings with fresh ingredients from her local markets. As a result, her dishes are not always strictly authentic but have an appealing originality. For the main courses of Menus 2 and 3, she calls for two varieties of seafood seldom used in Mexican kitchens: sole and scallops. To give the dishes a Mexican character, she seasons both with coriander, chilies, and garlic. Such flexibility makes her Mexican cooking unusual, and she counsels novice cooks to familiarize themselves with Mexican ingredients and then to be creative with them.

In her Menu 1 brunch, which features chorizo omelets, she combines elements of two popular Mexican egg recipes—*huevos rancheros* (fried eggs with a spicy tomato sauce), and eggs scrambled with chorizo sausage. The omelets are folded over an avocado, grated cheese, and chorizo filling, then served with a sauce of red bell peppers, tomato, and chilies.

For this celebratory brunch, serve each guest an omelet filled to overflowing and a tall glass of iced fruit punch. Place a bowl of the tomato-chili sauce and a basket of warm tortillas within easy reach. The colorful components of this meal make a dazzling centerpiece for the table.

73

Chorizo Omelets with Tomato-Chili Sauce
Steamed Tortillas
Fruit Refresco

Cooking a successful omelet takes less than a minute. For fluffy omelets, bring the eggs to room temperature before using them. To keep the beaten eggs from sticking to the pan, a nonstick or well-seasoned pan is essential. The perfect utensil is an omelet pan, specially designed for cooking omelets. Both the pan and the butter must be hot before you pour in the eggs. Heat the pan until a drop of water skitters on the surface, then add the butter, swirling it around until it foams. At this point, both the pan and the butter are ready. Because omelet-making takes so little time, have the rest of the meal prepared and your guests seated at the table before you cook the omelets.

WHAT TO DRINK

The cook suggests an icy pitcher of sangria if you are not making the Fruit Refresco.

SHOPPING LIST AND STAPLES

½ pound mild chorizo or ground-pork breakfast sausage
Small avocado
2 medium-size red bell peppers
Small head iceberg lettuce
Large tomato (about ¾ pound)
Small bunch scallions
2 fresh red or green chilies, or 1½ teaspoons crushed red pepper flakes
Medium-size bunch fresh mint
Small lemon or 1 tablespoon red wine vinegar
2 large limes (optional)
1 papaya, 1 mango, 2 oranges, 1 banana, small pineapple, small canteloupe, small honeydew, or watermelon in any combination of four
8 large eggs
1 stick unsalted butter, approximately
½ pound Monterey Jack cheese
8 fresh corn or flour tortillas, or 1 package frozen
7¼-ounce can black olives for garnish (optional)
6-ounce can tomato paste
2 tablespoons olive oil
½ cup superfine sugar, approximately
1 teaspoon granulated sugar
1 teaspoon chili powder
1 tablespoon dried oregano
Salt
¼ cup white rum (optional)

UTENSILS

Food processor or blender
Medium-size skillet
Medium-size saucepan
7-inch omelet pan
Medium-size bowl
Small bowl
Large pitcher
Salad spinner (optional)
Measuring cups and spoons
Chef's knife
Paring knife
Wooden spoon
Slotted spoon
Metal spatula
Whisk
Grater

START-TO-FINISH STEPS

One hour ahead: If using frozen tortillas, set out to thaw.

1. Follow tortillas recipe step 1.
2. Follow omelets recipe steps 1 and 2 and chili sauce recipe steps 1 and 2.
3. Follow fruit recipe steps 1 through 4.
4. Follow chili sauce recipe step 3 and tortillas recipe steps 2 and 3.
5. Follow chili sauce recipe step 4 and omelets recipe steps 3 through 5.
6. Follow chili sauce recipe step 5 and fruit recipe step 5.
7. Follow chili sauce recipe step 6, tortillas recipe step 4, fruit recipe step 6, omelet recipe steps 6 through 8, and serve.

RECIPES

Chorizo Omelets with Tomato-Chili Sauce

½ pound Monterey Jack cheese
Small bunch scallions
2 large limes for garnish (optional)
Small head iceberg lettuce
½ pound mild chorizo or ground-pork breakfast sausage
Small avocado
4 to 8 tablespoons unsalted butter
8 large eggs

1 teaspoon chili powder
Salt
Tomato-Chili Sauce (see following recipe)
8 black olives for garnish (optional)

1. Grate enough cheese to measure 2 cups. Wash scallions, trim, and pat dry. Chop enough to measure ¼ cup. Slice limes for garnish, if using.
2. Separate lettuce leaves, wash and dry in salad spinner or pat dry with paper towels. Shred enough lettuce to measure 4 cups.
3. Remove casing from sausage and crumble meat into medium-size skillet. Break up chorizo or sausage meat with wooden spoon, and cook, stirring occasionally, over medium heat 5 to 7 minutes, or until chorizo is cooked through. Drain fat from pan and set chorizo aside in warm place.
4. While chorizo is cooking, combine cheese and scallions in medium-size bowl.
5. Peel and pit avocado. Cut into ½- to ¾-inch dice.
6. To make omelets: Melt 2 tablespoons butter in omelet pan over medium heat. While butter is melting, break 2 eggs into small bowl. Add ¼ teaspoon chili powder, 2 tablespoons water, and a dash of salt. With whisk or fork, beat just to combine eggs with other ingredients; do not overbeat.
7. Raise heat under pan to medium-high. When butter foams, add eggs and cook, using spatula to lift edges so that uncooked egg flows underneath omelet. When omelet has set but center is still moist, about 1 minute, top with avocado, cheese, and chorizo. Fold omelet in half and slide onto dinner plate, taking care not to spill filling in pan. Top omelet with shredded lettuce and tomato-chili sauce, and garnish with lime slices and olives, if desired. Serve omelet and repeat procedure for remaining omelets, adding butter as necessary.
8. Serve omelets with bowl of remaining chili sauce.

Tomato-Chili Sauce

2 medium-size red bell peppers
Large tomato (about ¾ pound)
2 fresh red or green chilies, washed and patted dry, or
    1½ teaspoons crushed red pepper flakes
2 tablespoons olive oil
1 tablespoon tomato paste
1 tablespoon lemon juice or red wine vinegar
1 tablespoon dried oregano, crumbled
1 teaspoon sugar

1. Wash red bell peppers and pat dry. Halve, core, seed, and dice peppers. Wash tomato, pat dry, and dice.
2. Prepare chilies (see page 9). Chop enough to measure 2 tablespoons; set aside.
3. Heat olive oil in medium-size saucepan over medium-high heat. Add bell peppers, tomatoes, and chilies or crushed red pepper flakes, and sauté, stirring, about 3 minutes.
4. Add ½ cup water, tomato paste, lemon juice, oregano, and sugar, and stir until blended. Bring to a simmer and

cook 10 minutes, stirring occasionally.
5. Remove sauce from heat, cover, and keep warm until ready to serve.
6. Stir sauce to recombine and transfer extra to bowl.

Steamed Tortillas

8 corn or flour tortillas

1. Preheat oven to 300 degrees.
2. Stack tortillas and wrap first in barely damp dish towel, and then in aluminum foil.
3. Place tortillas in oven until heated through and soft, 10 to 15 minutes.
4. Remove tortillas from wrapping and transfer to napkin-lined basket.

Fruit Refresco

1 papaya, 1 mango, 2 oranges, 1 banana, small pineapple, or small canteloupe, honeydew, or watermelon in any combination of four
½ to 1 cup fresh mint leaves
¼ to ½ cup superfine sugar, approximately
¼ cup white rum (optional)

1. Peel fruit of your choice and cut enough into chunks to measure 1 cup each.
2. Stem mint leaves, wash, and pat dry.
3. Place fruit and mint leaves in food processor or blender and process until puréed.
4. Transfer fruit mixture to large pitcher and refrigerate.
5. Stir 1 quart water into fruit mixture and add sugar to taste. Add ice and rum, if desired, and stir.
6. Serve over ice in tall glasses.

ADDED TOUCH

A rich hot-chocolate drink is a satisfying cold-weather alternative to the fruit refresco.

Vanilla Chocolate

4 ounces semi-sweet chocolate
1 pint half-and-half
1 pint milk
2 tablespoons vanilla extract
Dash of nutmeg
4 cinnamon sticks

1. Break chocolate into pieces and place in medium-size heavy-gauge saucepan. Melt chocolate over low heat, stirring occasionally.
2. When chocolate has melted, add half-and-half and milk, stirring until blended.
3. Heat mixture gently just until it begins to steam. Do not let it come to a boil.
4. Remove hot chocolate from heat and stir in vanilla extract and nutmeg. Using whisk or electric mixer, beat mixture until frothy.
5. Pour mixture into mugs and serve garnished with cinnamon sticks.

Fillet of Sole with Almonds
Mexican Rice
Jícama Salad

This simple dinner of fillets of sole accompanied by rice and salad is a year-round meal that is perfect for company. When Vickie Simms devised the menu, she chose a familiar fish and starch but introduced jícama, an unusual vegetable indigenous to Mexico (see page 12). Many supermarkets now carry whole or cut-up jícama.

The sauce for the sautéed fillets contains sliced toasted almonds. To prevent rancidity, store untoasted almonds in a tightly covered container or plastic bag in the refrigerator or in the freezer.

Fillets of sole garnished with toasted almonds and rice cooked with tomato make up a simple, yet elegant dinner. Serve the jícama salad as a side dish and garnish it with black olives and walnuts, if you wish.

WHAT TO DRINK

Choose a white wine of some substance, such as a California Sauvignon Blanc or Chardonnay, for this menu.

SHOPPING LIST AND STAPLES

1½ to 2 pounds fillets of sole
1 pound jícama
Small head red-leaf lettuce
Medium-size tomato (about ½ pound)
2 medium-size onions
2 large cloves garlic
4 serrano chilies, or 4-ounce can peeled green chilies
Small bunch coriander

Small bunch chives (optional)
2 limes
Medium-size orange
2 eggs
3 tablespoons unsalted butter
2 cups chicken stock, preferably homemade
  (see page 13), or canned
7¼-ounce can whole black olives (optional)
4-ounce can walnut halves (optional)
¼ cup olive oil
2 tablesoons walnut oil
3½-ounce can sliced almonds
1 cup long-grain white rice
1 teaspoon chili powder
Salt and freshly ground black pepper

UTENSILS

Large skillet
Medium-size saucepan with cover
Small saucepan
Pie plate
15 x 10-inch baking pan
Medium-size bowl
4 heatproof dinner plates
4 salad plates
Salad spinner (optional)
Measuring cups and spoons
Chef's knife
Paring knife
Wooden spoon

Metal spatula
Grater
Juicer
Garlic press
Zester
Rubber gloves (optional)

START-TO-FINISH STEPS

1. Peel and chop onion, and peel and press or mince garlic for sole and rice recipes.
2. Follow sole recipe step 1 and salad recipe steps 1 through 4.
3. Follow rice recipe steps 1 through 5.
4. While rice is cooking, follow sole recipe steps 2 through 8.
5. Follow rice recipe steps 6 through 8.
6. Follow sole recipe steps 9 and 10.
7. Follow salad recipe step 5, sole recipe step 11, rice recipe step 9, and serve.

RECIPES

Fillet of Sole with Almonds

1 cup sliced almonds
¼ cup coriander leaves
4 fresh serrano chilies, washed, patted dry, and seeded, or 4-ounce can peeled green chilies, rinsed, drained, and patted dry
2 limes
1½ to 2 pounds fillets of sole
Salt
Freshly ground black pepper
2 eggs
3 tablespoons unsalted butter
2 tablespoons olive oil
½ cup chopped onion
Large clove garlic

1. Preheat oven to 350 degrees.
2. Place almonds on baking sheet and toast in oven, shaking them frequently to prevent scorching, 5 to 8 minutes, or until edges of almonds have turned brown.
3. While almonds are toasting, wash coriander and pat dry. Coarsely chop enough to measure ¼ cup; set aside.
4. Prepare chilies (see pages 9, 10). Chop and set aside.
5. Using zester, make enough lime zest to measure 1 tablespoon and squeeze enough lime to measure 2 tablespoons juice.
6. Remove almonds from oven; set aside. Reduce oven temperature to 250 degrees.
7. Wipe sole with damp paper towels and sprinkle with salt and pepper to taste.
8. Break eggs into pie plate and beat lightly.
9. Heat butter and oil in large skillet and over medium-high heat. Dip 2 fillets in beaten egg, let excess drip off, and place fillets in pan. Cook 2 to 3 minutes per side, until egg is cooked and golden. Transfer to dinner plates and keep warm in oven. Repeat process with remaining fillets.

10. For sauce, add onion, garlic, and chilies to butter and oil remaining in pan and sauté, stirring, about 1 minute. Add lime juice, lime zest, and coriander, and stir to combine.
11. Remove plates from oven and spoon sauce over sole. Sprinkle with toasted almonds and serve immediately.

Mexican Rice

Medium-size tomato (about ½ pound)
2 tablespoons olive oil
1 cup long-grain white rice
2 cups chicken stock, approximately
1 cup chopped onion
Large clove garlic, pressed or minced
Small bunch chives for garnish (optional)

1. Core, halve, and seed tomato. Chop coarsely and set aside.
2. Heat oil in medium-size saucepan over medium-high heat. Add rice and sauté, stirring frequently, about 2 to 3 minutes, or just until golden.
3. While sautéing rice, bring chicken stock to a boil over medium heat in small saucepan.
4. Add onion and garlic to rice, and sauté, stirring frequently, about 5 minutes, or until onion is soft. Stir in chopped tomato.
5. Add 1¾ cups hot stock to rice mixture. Stir rice once, adjust heat to a simmer, cover, and cook 18 minutes, or until liquid is absorbed and rice is tender.
6. Taste rice to check for doneness. If not quite cooked, add remaining ¼ cup stock, recover pan, and cook until absorbed.
7. Let rice stand, covered, 10 minutes before serving.
8. Wash chives, if using, and pat dry. Chop enough to measure 2 tablespoons.
9. Divide rice among dinner plates and garnish with chopped chives, if desired.

Jícama Salad

Medium-size orange
1 pound jícama
Small head red leaf lettuce
2 tablespoons walnut oil
1 teaspoon chili powder
½ cup walnut halves for garnish (optional)
12 whole black olives for garnish (optional)

1. Squeeze enough orange juice to measure ¼ cup. Grate enough peel to measure 1 tablespoon, if desired.
2. Peel jícama and julienne enough to measure ¾ cup.
3. Combine orange juice, walnut oil, chili powder, and orange peel, if using, in medium-size bowl. Add jícama and toss with dressing. Cover and refrigerate.
4. Separate lettuce into leaves, wash, and dry in salad spinner or pat dry with paper towels. Line 4 salad plates with lettuce. Cover and refrigerate.
5. Toss salad to recombine and divide among individual salad plates. If desired, garnish with walnut halves and olives.

Lime Soup with Tortillas
Fiery Scallops with Mango Relish
Tomato and Cheese Salad Vinaigrette

Bright pottery provides a lively background for the scallops, mango relish, and salad of lettuce, tomato slices, and grated cheese. Lemon and lime wheels and chopped coriander decorate the lime soup.

A bowl of steaming lime soup with crisp tortilla strips is a regular feature of Yucatecan menus. For her version, Vickie Simms bakes rather than fries the tortilla strips.

To make the mango relish served with the scallops, select mangos that are mature but not soft, so that the cubed fruit retains its shape. (For further information about mangos, see page 12.)

WHAT TO DRINK

A well-chilled, crisp, dry white wine, such as a Verdicchio or Muscadet, would take some of the "fire" out of the scallops with mango relish.

SHOPPING LIST AND STAPLES

1½ pounds sea scallops or prawns
3 large tomatoes (about 1½ pounds total weight), plus
   2 small tomatoes (about ½ pound total weight)
Small head Romaine lettuce
Medium-size onion
6 large cloves garlic
Small bunch scallions
2 serrano chilies, plus 4 serrano or jalapeño chilies
Small bunch coriander
2 lemons
6 limes
2 small oranges
2 small mangos
Small hard apple, preferably Granny Smith
4 tablespoons unsalted butter, approximately
¼ pound Monterey Jack cheese
8 fresh corn tortillas, or 1 package frozen
6 cups chicken stock, preferably homemade
   (see page 13), or canned
¼ cup olive oil, approximately
¼ cup plus 1 tablespoon vegetable oil
¼ cup raspberry vinegar, preferably, or cider vinegar
⅓ cup white wine vinegar
1 teaspoon dried oregano
½ teaspoon ground cumin
Salt and freshly ground black pepper

UTENSILS

Large skillet
Medium-size saucepan

11 x 17-inch cookie sheet
Medium-size bowl
Small bowl
Salad spinner (optional)
Measuring cups and spoons
Chef's knife
Paring knife
Ladle
Slotted spoon
Wooden spoon
Grater
Juicer
Garlic press (optional)
Small jar with tight-fitting lid
Rubber gloves

START-TO-FINISH STEPS

1. Prepare tomatoes for soup and scallops recipes. Prepare scallions for scallops and salad recipes. Prepare coriander for soup and scallops recipes. Prepare garlic for soup, scallops, and salad recipes. Squeeze lime juice for soup and relish recipes, and squeeze lemon juice for scallops recipe.
2. Follow relish recipe steps 1 through 5.
3. Follow soup recipe steps 1 through 5.
4. While soup is simmering, follow scallops recipe step 1 and salad recipe steps 1 through 4.
5. Follow soup recipe steps 6 and 7, and serve.
6. Follow scallops recipe steps 2 and 3, and salad recipe steps 5 and 6.
7. Follow scallops recipe steps 4 through 6 and serve with salad.

RECIPES

Lime Soup with Tortillas

8 stale corn tortillas
Medium-size onion
1 lemon
1 lime
1 tablespoon vegetable oil
3½ cups seeded and chopped tomatoes
3 large cloves garlic, pressed or minced
1 to 2 fresh serrano chilies, washed and patted dry
6 cups chicken stock
½ teaspoon ground cumin
Salt

⅓ cup freshly squeezed lime juice
¼ cup chopped coriander

1. Preheat oven to 300 degrees.
2. Cut tortillas into ½-inch-wide strips. Peel onion and slice into rounds. Grate enough lemon zest to measure 1 teaspoon, and cut lemon and lime into four ¼-inch-thick slices. Prepare chilies (see page 9) and slice.
3. Arrange tortilla strips in single layer on cookie sheet and bake until crisp, about 10 minutes.
4. While tortillas are baking, heat oil in medium-size saucepan over medium-high heat. Add onion, tomatoes, garlic, and chilies, and sauté, stirring frequently, about 3 minutes, or until onions are translucent.
5. Add stock and cumin, and bring to a boil. Reduce to a simmer, and cook, uncovered, 10 minutes.
6. Remove pan from heat, add salt to taste, and stir in lime juice and lemon zest. Divide tortilla strips among 4 soup bowls and ladle soup over strips.
7. Garnish each bowl with a slice each of lemon and lime, and a sprinkling of coriander.

Fiery Scallops with Mango Relish

2 to 4 serrano or jalapeño chilies
¼ cup minced scallions
4 tablespoons unsalted butter, approximately
¼ cup olive oil, approximately
2 large cloves garlic, pressed or finely minced
1½ pounds sea scallops
¼ cup plus 1 tablespoon seeded and chopped tomato
Salt
2 to 4 tablespoons freshly squeezed lemon juice
1 tablespoon chopped coriander for garnish
Mango Relish (see following recipe)

1. Wash chilies, pat dry, and split in half lengthwise. Seed and devein (see page 9).
2. Heat butter and oil in large skillet over medium heat. When butter has melted, add chilies and garlic, and sauté, stirring constantly, about 1 minute.
3. Add scallops, reduce heat to medium, and sauté, stirring and tossing, until scallops turn white and are cooked through, about 3 to 5 minutes.
4. With slotted spoon, divide scallops among dinner plates.
5. Working quickly, add scallions and tomatoes to sauce remaining in pan, along with more butter and oil, if pan is too dry. Cook, stirring, 1 to 2 minutes, just until heated

through. Add salt and lemon juice to taste, stir to combine, and spoon mixture over scallops.
6. Garnish scallops with chopped coriander and serve with Mango Relish.

Mango Relish

2 small mangos
2 small oranges
Small hard apple, preferably Granny Smith
1 lime
3 to 4 tablespoons lime juice
3 to 4 tablespoons raspberry vinegar, preferably, or cider vinegar

1. Peel mangos, remove pits, and cut flesh into dice.
2. Peel and dice oranges. Core and dice apple. Grate enough lime zest to measure 1 teaspoon.
3. Place diced fruit in medium-size bowl and toss to combine.
4. Combine lime juice and raspberry vinegar to taste in small bowl and beat until blended.
5. Pour dressing over fruit, sprinkle with lime zest, and toss gently.

Tomato and Cheese Salad Vinaigrette

Small head Romaine lettuce
2 small tomatoes (about ½ pound total weight)
3 tablespoons chopped scallions
¼ pound Monterey Jack cheese
1 clove garlic, pressed or finely chopped
¼ cup vegetable oil
⅓ cup white wine vinegar
1 teaspoon dried oregano, crumbled
Salt and freshly ground black pepper

1. Separate lettuce into leaves, wash, and dry in salad spinner or pat dry with paper towels. Tear lettuce into bite-size pieces. Wrap in paper twels and refrigerate.
2. Wash tomatoes, pat dry, and cut into ¼-inch-thick slices.
3. Grate enough cheese to measure 1 cup; set aside.
4. Combine scallions, garlic, oil, vinegar, oregano, and salt and pepper to taste in small jar with tight-fitting lid and shake until blended.
5. Make a bed of lettuce on each dinner plate, divide tomato slices among them, and top with cheese.
6. Shake dressing to recombine and pour over salad.

Lucinda Hutson

Lucinda Hutson was raised in the border town of El Paso, Texas, where she developed a love for fine Mexican food that was later heightened by her travels through the country. Today she uses her knowledge of Mexican cooking as a foundation for her own interpretive Mexican dishes, in which she eliminates frying when possible, utilizes fresh produce, and creates lively sauces. "I do not merely translate traditional recipes," she says. "Instead, I try to use traditional ingredients in an imaginative way." In Menu 1, for example, the main course of red snapper, or *huachinango*, is flavored with fresh ginger, an Asian rather than a Mexican seasoning, yet the dish is still traditionally *al mojo de ajo*—smothered with garlic.

Fresh produce, unusual combinations of herbs and spices (she urges serious Mexican cooks to grow their own herbs), as well as unique garnishes are essential to her cooking. In Menu 2, her green chili casserole, a variation on the standard *chiles rellenos* (stuffed chilies), calls for fresh Anaheim or *poblano* chilies garnished with sliced avocado and onion rings.

The spicy shrimp and spinach soup of Menu 3, a recipe the cook learned from a fisherman from the Gulf Coast state of Veracruz, is filled with herbs. When served with a crusty garlic bread, this soup-and-salad meal is perfect for lunch.

Broiled red snapper, flavored with ginger, garlic, coriander and crushed red pepper, is a light main course for a company dinner. A colorful salad of citrus sections with pomegranate seeds, avocado slices, and red onion rings on red leaf lettuce may be served with the fish or after.

Marinated Red Snapper
Citrus Salad with Pomegranate Seeds

The marinade for the main-course fish calls for a dash of gold tequila, which has a richer flavor than white tequila. You can substitute white tequila, however, or omit the liquor altogether, adding more lime juice if you do so.

Pomegranates come to market in the fall or early winter. If unavailable, fresh raspberries make an excellent substitute.

This is a light, refreshing meal, but to provide for larger appetites, you may want to extend it by adding rice or a basket of warm tortillas with butter on the side.

WHAT TO DRINK

Tequila gimlets (3 ounces tequila, plus 2 ounces freshly squeezed lime juice, over ice) would be a perfect drink to precede the citrus flavors of this menu; serve beer or ale with the meal itself.

SHOPPING LIST AND STAPLES

4 fillets of fresh red snapper, flounder, or any
  light white fish (about ½ pound each)
Medium-size avocado
1 head red leaf lettuce
Small bunch radishes (optional)
Medium-size red onion
Small bunch coriander
3 to 4 large cloves garlic
2-inch piece fresh ginger
Large pink or ruby red grapefruit (about 1½ pounds)
2 navel oranges
4 limes, plus 1 lime (optional)
1 fresh pomegranate, or 1 cup fresh raspberries
1 cup vegetable oil
3 tablespoons olive oil
5 tablespoons red wine vinegar
¼ cup granulated sugar
1 teaspoon dry mustard
½ teaspoon pure chili powder or paprika
¼ teaspoon crushed red pepper flakes
Salt and freshly ground pepper
1 tablespoon gold tequila (optional)

UTENSILS

Food processor or blender
Broiler pan

13 × 9 × 2-inch glass baking dish
Medium-size bowl
Small bowl
Salad spinner (optional)
Measuring cups and spoons
Chef's knife
Paring knife
Wide metal spatula
Fork
Vegetable peeler
Grater

START-TO-FINISH STEPS

1. Juice limes for salad and for snapper recipes.
2. Follow snapper recipe steps 1 through 4.
3. Follow salad recipe steps 1 through 8.
4. Follow snapper recipe steps 5 through 7.
5. While fish is broiling, follow salad recipe steps 9 through 12.
6. Follow snapper recipe step 8 and serve with salad.

RECIPES

Marinated Red Snapper

2-inch piece fresh ginger
3 to 4 cloves garlic
Small bunch coriander
¼ cup freshly squeezed lime juice
¼ teaspoon crushed red pepper flakes
1 tablespoon gold tequila (optional)
3 tablespoons olive oil
4 fillets of fresh red snapper, flounder, or any light
  white fish (about ½ pound each)
1 lime for garnish (optional)
4 to 6 radishes for garnish (optional)
Salt and freshly ground pepper
½ teaspoon pure chili powder or paprika

1. Peel and grate ginger. Peel and mince garlic.
2. Wash coriander and pat dry with paper towels. Chop enough to measure ¼ cup.
3. In glass baking dish, combine ginger, garlic, coriander, lime juice, red pepper, and tequila, if using, and beat with fork until blended. Add oil and beat again.
4. Place fillets in dish, turning once to coat with marinade.

Cover with plastic wrap and marinate at room temperature 30 to 40 minutes, turning occasionally.

5. Preheat broiler. Line broiler pan with foil.

6. Slice lime into 8 thin wedges, if using. Wash radishes, if using, and cut into ⅛-inch-thick slices.

7. Arrange fillets in single layer on foil-lined broiler pan set 4 to 6 inches from heating element. Cook 3 to 6 minutes per side, or until fish can be flaked easily with fork. Watch fish carefully to prevent overcooking—the longer fish has marinated, the more rapidly it will cook.

8. Transfer fish fillets to individual dinner plates and sprinkle with salt, pepper, and chili powder or paprika to taste. Serve garnished with lime wedges and radish slices, if desired.

Citrus Salad with Pomegranate Seeds

Medium-size red onion
1 lime
2 navel oranges
¼ cup granulated sugar
1 teaspoon dry mustard
5 tablespoons red wine vinegar
2 tablespoons freshly squeezed lime juice
¼ teaspoon salt
1 cup vegetable oil
Large pink or ruby red grapefruit (about 1½ pounds)
1 fresh pomegranate, or 1 cup fresh raspberries
1 head red leaf lettuce
Medium-size avocado

1. Peel onion, halve, and coarsely chop one half. Slice remaining half into ¼-inch-thick slices. Separate slices into rings, wrap in plastic, and refrigerate.

2. Using coarse side of grater, grate citrus rind.

3. In bowl of food processor or blender, combine chopped onion, grated rind, sugar, mustard, vinegar, 1 tablespoon lime juice, and salt, and process until puréed. (If using blender, citrus peel may not entirely dissolve into purée. If it does not, simply blend until it is as finely chopped as possible.)

4. With processor or blender running, drizzle in oil until dressing begins to thicken. Then gradually add remaining oil in a slow, steady stream. When oil has been completely incorporated, taste dressing and adjust seasoning, if necessary. Cover bowl or blender jar and refrigerate. Dressing will continue to thicken as it chills.

5. Peel grapefruit and oranges, removing as much white pith as possible. Section fruit by cutting between membranes; discard membranes. Place fruit in medium-size bowl and set aside.

6. If using pomegranate, cut gash in rind and, using thumbs, pry fruit open. Break into smaller sections to facilitate removal of seeds. Using your fingers, gently separate seeds with the juicy red pulp surrounding them from the hard rind; discard rind. Separate seeds from one another. If using raspberries, rinse in cool water and gently pat dry with paper towels. Add pomegranate seeds

or raspberries to bowl with citrus fruit. Cover with plastic wrap and refrigerate until needed.

7. Wash lettuce and dry in salad spinner or pat dry with paper towels. Roll lettuce in paper towels or place in plastic bag and refrigerate until needed.

8. Place individual serving plates in refrigerator to chill.

9. Just before serving, peel avocado and cut in half lengthwise. Twist to separate halves; remove and discard pit. Slice avocado into ½-inch-thick crescents (see page 12). Place in small bowl and toss with remaining tablespoon lime juice.

10. Remove plates and salad ingredients from refrigerator. Line plates with lettuce leaves.

11. Gently toss citrus sections and pomegranate seeds or raspberries until combined. Add avocado and toss.

12. Divide salad among lettuce-lined plates. Top each portion with onion rings and dressing.

ADDED TOUCH

If Mexican chocolate is difficult to find, make your own (see page 13).

Mexican Chocolate Ice Cream

2 squares unsweetened chocolate
3 squares Mexican chocolate
3 egg yolks
Pinch salt
1 cup granulated sugar
1 cup milk
2 cups heavy cream
Cinnamon
½ teaspoon vanilla extract
¼ teaspoon pure almond extract
½ cup toasted, slivered almonds for garnish (optional)

1. Grate both chocolates over waxed paper and set aside.

2. In medium-size bowl, beat egg yolks and salt with electric mixer at high speed 1 or 2 minutes, or until thickened. Reduce speed to medium, and gradually add sugar. Increase speed to high and continue to beat 2 to 3 minutes, or until yolks are pale yellow and fluffy.

3. Combine milk and cream in medium-size saucepan and heat over medium heat just until bubbles form at the edge and mixture starts to simmer. Immediately remove pan from heat.

4. Gradually add scalded milk-cream mixture to yolk mixture, stirring constantly until completely incorporated.

5. Return mixture to saucepan and cook, stirring constantly with whisk, over low heat 3 to 5 minutes, or until thick enough to coat the back of a spoon. (Watch mixture very carefully. Do not permit to boil or eggs will curdle.)

6. Remove custard from heat and stir in grated chocolate, ¼ teaspoon cinnamon, and vanilla and almond extracts. Continue to stir until chocolate has completely melted.

7. Place mixture in canister of ice-cream maker and proceed according to manufacturer's directions.

8. To serve, sprinkle each portion of ice cream with cinnamon or toasted slivered almonds, if desired.

Green Chili Casserole with Sweet-and-Spicy Tomato Sauce
Orange and Melon Salad with Mint Marinade
Mexican Corn Muffins

For this buffet-style brunch, serve the green chili casserole from its baking dish and offer the tomato sauce in a separate pitcher.

An orange and melon salad and corn muffins with raisins and pine nuts round out the meal.

The green chili casserole is a variation on the classic Mexican dish, *chiles rellenos*, or cheese-filled batter-dipped green chilies that are fried. The accompanying tomato sauce for the casserole contains cinnamon, a southern Mexico influence. If you do not use fresh chilies for the casserole, combine the optional fresh jalapeños with the canned mild chilies for a more piquant flavor.

WHAT TO DRINK

For an unusual combination of flavors, serve a German Riesling with this menu. A Mosel, with its delicacy, fruitiness, and touch of sweetness, is another good choice.

SHOPPING LIST AND STAPLES

Small avocado (optional)
Small head red leaf lettuce
Medium-size red onion (optional)
2 bunches scallions
Small bunch fresh mint, or small bunch parsley plus
    3 tablespoons dried mint
4 large cloves garlic, plus 1 clove (optional)
6 fresh poblano or Anaheim chilies, or two 4-ounce cans
    whole green chilies
1 or 2 fresh jalapeños (optional)
Medium-size cantaloupe or honeydew, or large papaya or
    mango
3 medium-size navel oranges
4 limes
15-ounce can tomato sauce
6 eggs
½ pint half-and-half or milk
1 stick plus 2 tablespoons unsalted butter
¼ pound Monterey Jack cheese
¼ pound sharp yellow Cheddar cheese
¼ cup safflower oil
¼ teaspoon vanilla extract
½ cup plus ½ tablespoon flour
⅔ cup yellow cornmeal
1½ teaspoons baking powder
¼ teaspoon baking soda
¾ cup plus 2 teaspoons dark brown sugar, approximately,
    or ½ cup honey plus 2 teaspoons dark brown sugar
9-ounce package dark raisins
3-ounce jar pine nuts, or 4-ounce can blanched, slivered
    almonds
1 teaspoon pure chili powder
1 teaspoon ground cinnamon
1 teaspoon ground coriander seed
1 teaspoon dry mustard
Salt and freshly ground pepper
¼ cup dry sherry

UTENSILS

Medium-size saucepan
9½ × 9½-inch baking/serving dish
12-cup muffin tin
Large bowl
4 medium-size bowls
Small bowl
Platter
Salad spinner (optional)
Measuring cups and spoons
Chef's knife
Paring knife
Long-handled wooden spoon
Slotted spoon
Rubber spatula
Fork
Electric mixer
Grater
Melon baller (optional)
Cake tester or toothpick

START-TO-FINISH STEPS

One hour ahead: Remove butter for muffins from refrigerator and prepare chilies (see pages 9, 10) for casserole recipe.

1. Preheat oven to 350 degrees.
2. Peel and mince garlic and prepare scallions for chili casserole, tomato sauce, and salad, if using.
3. Follow salad recipe steps 1 through 5.
4. Follow muffins recipe steps 1 through 9.
5. Follow casserole recipe steps 1 through 8.
6. Follow salad recipe step 6.
7. Follow sauce recipe steps 1 through 3.
8. While sauce simmers, follow casserole recipe step 8.
9. Follow muffins recipe step 10.
10. Follow salad recipe step 7, sauce recipe step 4, casserole recipe step 9, and serve with warm muffins.

RECIPES

Green Chili Casserole with Sweet-and-Spicy Tomato Sauce

6 fresh poblano or Anaheim chilies, roasted, peeled, and
    seeded, or two 4-ounce cans whole green chilies, rinsed
    drained, and patted dry
1 or 2 fresh jalapeños (optional), washed and patted dry
1½ tablespoons minced garlic
½ cup minced scallions, plus ¼ cup for garnish (optional)
¼ pound Monterey Jack cheese
¼ pound sharp yellow Cheddar cheese
½ tablespoon flour
4 eggs, separated
⅓ cup half-and-half or milk
Salt and freshly ground pepper
Small avocado for garnish (optional)
Medium-size red onion for garnish (optional)
½ teaspoon pure chili powder for garnish (optional)
Sweet-and-Spicy Tomato Sauce (see following recipe)

1. Cut prepared chilies into 2-inch-long strips.
2. Butter baking dish. Place chilies in dish, add minced

garlic and scallions, and toss to combine.

3. Grate cheeses and sprinkle over chili mixture.

4. Sprinkle flour over egg yolks and beat until blended. Add half-and-half and salt and pepper to taste, and beat until incorporated. Wash and dry beaters.

5. Starting at slow and increasing speed to medium as egg whites begin to foam, beat whites until peaks form and whites are stiff but not dry.

6. Using rubber spatula, fold whites into yolks and gently turn into baking dish. With fork, gently swirl through egg layer to combine eggs with chili mixture.

7. Bake, uncovered, in 350-degree oven 25 to 30 minutes, or until crust is deeply golden.

8. Prepare remaining garnishes, if using: Peel and halve avocado lengthwise. Remove and discard pit. Cut into ½-inch-thick crescents (see page 12). Peel onion and cut into ⅛-inch-thick slices. Separate into rings.

9. Remove casserole from oven and garnish with chili powder, avocado slices, red onion rings, and chopped scallions, if desired. Serve with Sweet-and-Spicy Tomato Sauce on the side.

Sweet-and-Spicy Tomato Sauce

2 tablespoons unsalted butter
¾ cup chopped scallions
1½ tablespoons minced garlic
15-ounce can tomato sauce
1½ teaspoons dark brown sugar
½ teaspoon ground cinnamon
¼ cup dry sherry

1. In medium-size saucepan, melt butter over medium heat. Add scallions and garlic, and sauté, stirring, 2 minutes, or until scallions are translucent.

2. Stir in tomato sauce, brown sugar, cinnamon, and ¼ cup water. Bring mixture to a boil and cook over high heat, stirring constantly, 2 minutes. Reduce heat to medium-high and simmer, stirring occasionally, 3 minutes.

3. Stir in sherry and simmer another 5 minutes.

4. Transfer sauce to small pitcher or bowl, sprinkle with cinnamon, and serve with green chili casserole.

Orange and Melon Salad with Mint Marinade

3 medium-size navel oranges
1 clove garlic (optional)
½ cup fresh mint leaves, or 3 tablespoons crushed dried
    mint and 3 tablespoons chopped parsley
3 tablespoons freshly squeezed lime juice
Medium-size cantaloupe or honeydew, or large papaya or
    mango, scooped into balls or cut into 1-inch chunks
1 teaspoon ground coriander seed
1 teaspoon dry mustard
1 teaspoon pure chili powder
½ teaspoon dark brown sugar, approximately
¼ cup safflower oil
Small head red leaf lettuce
¼ cup chopped scallion greens for garnish (optional)
Mint sprigs for garnish (optional)

1. Wash oranges and pat dry. On fine side of grater, grate rind of 2 oranges, avoiding white pith. Remove as much of remaining white pith as possible and cut oranges crosswise into ⅛- to ¼-inch-thick rounds.

2. If using garlic, peel and bruise clove by placing under flat of knife and leaning on blade with the heel of your hand. Prepare mint or parsley.

3. Scoop out melon or cut fruit into 1-inch chunks.

4. For marinade, combine orange rind, orange slices, lime juice, garlic, if using, coriander, dry mustard, chili powder, mint, and ½ teaspoon brown sugar (or to taste) in medium-size bowl. Add oil and stir with fork until blended. With back of spoon, mash mint.

5. Add melon to bowl and toss until evenly coated. Cover with plastic wrap and refrigerate, stirring occasionally, until ready to serve.

6. Wash lettuce and dry in salad spinner or pat dry with paper towels. Line platter with lettuce leaves. Cover with plastic wrap and refrigerate until ready to serve.

7. Remove garlic clove from fruit mixture and discard. Toss fruit with marinade and, with slotted spoon, transfer to lettuce-lined platter. Serve garnished with scallion greens and mint sprigs, if desired.

Mexican Corn Muffins

1 stick unsalted butter, at room temperature
2 medium-size limes
¾ cup dark brown sugar, or ½ cup honey
½ teaspoon ground cinnamon
¼ teaspoon vanilla extract
½ cup flour
⅔ cup yellow cornmeal
1½ teaspoons baking powder
¼ teaspoon baking soda
2 eggs
½ cup half-and-half or milk
⅓ cup dark raisins
½ cup pine nuts or blanched slivered almonds

1. Butter 12-cup muffin tin.

2. Grate rind of both limes, avoiding white pith.

3. In large bowl, cream butter. Add sugar or honey and beat until mixture is light and fluffy. Beat in grated rind, cinnamon, and vanilla extract.

4. Combine flour, cornmeal, baking powder, and baking soda in medium-size bowl, and stir with fork until blended.

5. In small bowl, beat eggs just until combined. Add half-and-half or milk and stir until blended.

6. To butter mixture, gradually add egg mixture, alternating additions with small amounts of flour mixture and beating after each addition until thoroughly combined.

7. When eggs and flour have been completely incorporated, beat in raisins and nuts.

8. Divide batter evenly among cups of muffin tin, filling each about two-thirds full.

9. Bake muffins in 350-degree oven about 30 to 35 minutes, or until golden and crusty around edges and cake tester or toothpick inserted in center comes out clean.

10. Transfer muffins to napkin-lined basket.

Spicy Shrimp and Spinach Soup
Stuffed Tomato Salad

The zesty shrimp and spinach soup is accompanied by tomato halves stuffed with corn, zucchini, and peppers.

The key to this soup is homemade chicken stock. Canned stock will work, but the soup will be less savory. If using canned stock, try using half chicken stock and half bottled clam juice for more flavor. You can add the sautéed onions, garlic, spices, and jalapeños to the stock early in the day, then boil the shrimp and spinach at the last minute. Use fresh, unpeeled shrimp; their shells enhance the soup's flavor. Peel the shrimp with your fingers as you eat the soup; have extra plates on the table for the shells. Serve the soup garnished with several, or all, of the suggested condiments, or subsitute some of your own choosing.

WHAT TO DRINK

A good dark Mexican beer would be refreshing with the spicy shrimp soup.

SHOPPING LIST AND STAPLES

16 to 20 medium-size fresh shrimp (¾ to 1 pound total weight), unpeeled
½ pound fresh spinach
Medium-size head Bibb lettuce
Small avocado

89

8 small or 4 medium-size firm tomatoes (about 1 pound
total weight)
Small zucchini
Medium-size red or green bell pepper
2 medium-size white onions (about 1 pound total weight)
Large bunch scallions
1 to 2 fresh jalapeños, or 4-ounce can, whole
5 large cloves garlic
Large bunch coriander
Small bunch fresh mint
7 small limes
5 cups chicken stock, preferably homemade (see page 13),
or 2½ cups canned chicken stock and three 8-ounce
bottles clam juice
3 tablespoons unsalted butter
¼ pound Parmesan cheese
10-ounce package frozen corn
¼ cup olive oil
2 tablespoons red wine vinegar
1 teaspoon brown sugar
1 teaspoon dried oregano
½ teaspoon dried thyme
½ teaspoon ground cumin
¼ teaspoon crushed red pepper flakes
1 bay leaf
Salt and freshly ground pepper
¼ teaspoon freshly ground white pepper

UTENSILS

Medium-size skillet
2 medium-size saucepans, one with cover
Medium-size bowl
3 small bowls
2 plates
Salad spinner (optional)
Colander
Measuring cups and spoons
Chef's knife
Paring knife
Wooden spoon
Tablespoon
Teaspoon or melon baller
Grater

START-TO-FINISH STEPS

Thirty minutes ahead: Prepare chilies (see pages 9, 10) for
soup recipe. Set out frozen corn to thaw for salad recipe.

1. Peel and mince garlic for soup and for salad. Wash
scallions, coriander, and mint, and pat dry. Chop scallions
and coriander for soup and for salad. Chop mint for salad.
Squeeze lime juice for soup and for salad.
2. Follow soup recipe steps 1 through 4.
3. Follow salad recipe steps 1 through 8.
4. Follow soup recipe steps 5 through 10.
5. Follow salad recipe step 9, soup recipe step 11, and
serve.

RECIPES

Spicy Shrimp and Spinach Soup

1 to 2 fresh jalapeños, washed, patted dry, and seeded, or
1 to 2 whole canned jalapeños, rinsed, drained, and
seeded
2 medium-size white onions
3 tablespoons unsalted butter
3 large cloves garlic, minced
¾ teaspoon crushed dried oregano
½ teaspoon dried thyme
1 bay leaf
5 cups chicken stock, or 2½ cups canned chicken stock
and 2½ cups bottled clam juice
Small avocado
2 tablespoons fresh lime juice
½ cup freshly grated Parmesan cheese
4 cups fresh spinach, packed
16 to 20 medium-size shrimp (¾ to 1 pound total weight),
unpeeled
2 small limes
¼ teaspoon freshly ground white pepper
Salt
1 cup chopped coriander
½ cup chopped scallions

1. Chop prepared jalapeños finely. Peel and chop onion.
2. Melt butter in skillet over medium heat. Add jalapeños,
onions, and garlic, and cook, stirring, until onions are
translucent, about 3 minutes. Remove pan from heat.
3. Stir in oregano, thyme, and bay leaf.
4. In medium-size saucepan, bring stock to a boil over high
heat. Reduce to a simmer, add sautéed vegetables, and
return to a boil. Reduce heat and simmer 30 minutes.
5. Peel and halve avocado lengthwise. Remove and discard
pit. Cut into ½-inch dice. Place in small bowl and toss with
1 tablespoon lime juice. Grate Parmesan; set aside.
6. Wash spinach thoroughly in several changes of cold
water and drain in colander. Remove tough stems and
discard. Tear spinach into bite-size pieces.
7. Rinse shrimp under cold running water and drain. Remove legs and discard.
8. Increase heat under stock to high and return to a boil.
Add shrimp and cook about 3 minutes, just until they turn
bright pink and become firm.
9. While shrimp are cooking, quarter limes.
10. Turn off heat under shrimp. Stir in spinach and lime
juice, cover, and allow to steam 2 minutes. Season with
white pepper and salt to taste.
11. Serve soup in individual bowls garnished with avocado, coriander, scallions, Parmesan, and lime wedges.

Stuffed Tomato Salad

8 small or 4 firm medium-size tomatoes (about 1 pound
total weight)
Salt
2 large cloves garlic, minced

3 tablespoons fresh lime juice
2 tablespoons red wine vinegar
1 teaspoon brown sugar
¼ teaspoon crushed red pepper flakes
¼ teaspoon oregano
½ teaspoon ground cumin
¼ cup olive oil
3 to 4 tablespoons chopped mint
1 tablespoon chopped coriander
Freshly ground black pepper
Medium-size red or green bell pepper
Medium-size head Bibb lettuce
Small zucchini
½ cup chopped scallions
1½ cups corn kernels, thawed and drained but still chilled

1. Tomatoes may be used peeled or unpeeled. If peeling, bring 2 quarts salted water to a boil in medium-size saucepan. Plunge tomatoes into boiling water and blanch 30 seconds. Transfer tomatoes to colander, refresh under cold running water, and remove peel with your fingers. If using tomatoes unpeeled, wash and pat dry.
2. Cut off tomato tops about ½ to ¾ inch from top. With teaspoon or melon baller, hollow out tomatoes, leaving a ¼-inch-thick shell. Discard seeds and pulp. Reserve firm flesh and chop. Lightly salt tomato shells. Cover plate with a layer of paper towels and invert shells on toweling. Leave 5 minutes.
3. For dressing, combine garlic, lime juice, vinegar, sugar, red pepper flakes, oregano, and cumin in small bowl. Beating with fork until blended, drizzle in oil. Place mint and coriander in small bowl and mash with back of tablespoon to release flavor. Add to vinaigrette along with salt and pepper to taste and beat to combine.
4. Turn tomato shells upright and add about 1½ teaspoons vinaigrette to each if using 4 medium-size tomatoes, or ¾ teaspoon if using small ones. Roll dressing around inside and outside of tomato to coat. Place tomatoes on plate, cover with plastic wrap, and refrigerate.
5. Core, halve, and seed bell pepper. Chop and set aside.
6. Wash lettuce and dry in salad spinner or pat dry with paper towels. Wrap in paper towels and refrigerate.
7. Scrub zucchini, rinse, and pat dry. Cut into ¼-inch dice.
8. In medium-size bowl, combine reserved tomato flesh, zucchini, scallions, bell pepper, corn, and salt and pepper to taste. Add remaining vinaigrette and toss to combine. Cover with plastic wrap and refrigerate.
9. Just before serving, line 4 plates with lettuce. Remove tomatoes and corn mixture from refrigerator. Pour any vinaigrette that has accumulated around tomatoes into corn mixture. Fill tomato shells generously with the corn mixture. Divide among plates and serve.

ADDED TOUCH

By serving these chicken breasts on a bed of rice, you can **transform** this soup and salad lunch into a substantial dinner.

Chicken Breasts in Lemon-Wine Sauce

4 chicken breast halves (about 1¾ pounds, total weight)
3 medium-size lemons
Medium-size yellow onion
4 large cloves garlic
1 to 2 fresh or canned jalapeño peppers, chopped
2 tablespoons unsalted butter
2 tablespoons olive oil
Salt and freshly ground white pepper
¾ cup dry white wine
¼ teaspoon ground coriander
½ teaspoon dried oregano, crumbled
½ teaspoon ground allspice
½ cup chopped scallions
½ cup chopped coriander or parsley
4-ounce jar water-packed whole red pimientos, rinsed, drained, and cut into ¼-inch-thick strips.

1. Wash chicken breasts and pat dry with paper towels. Trim excess fat from chicken and discard.
2. Grate rind of 2 lemons. Cut lemons in half and juice. Set aside. Cut remaining lemon into thin slices for garnish. Wrap in plastic and refrigerate.
3. Peel and chop onion. Peel garlic and mince 2 cloves. Bruise remaining cloves by placing them under flat of knife and leaning down on knife with heel of your hand.
4. Prepare jalapeños (see page 9). If a less fiery flavor is desired, first cut in half lengthwise and remove seeds.
5. In medium-size sauté pan, heat butter and oil over medium heat. Add the 2 bruised garlic cloves and sauté about 3 minutes, stirring frequently, until garlic is golden brown. Remove garlic from pan and discard.
6. Place chicken breasts, skin side up, in pan, raise heat to medium-high, and cook about 5 minutes, or until golden brown. Turn pieces skin side down and cook another 4 minutes, or until golden brown. Remove pan from heat.
7. Season chicken with salt and white pepper to taste, and transfer to large, covered casserole.
8. Heat fat remaining in skillet over medium-high heat. Add onion, minced garlic, and jalapeños, and cook 3 to 4 minutes, stirring frequently, just until onion is translucent. Stir in half of grated rind and cook 30 seconds. Pour mixture over chicken in casserole.
9. Add wine, ¼ cup water, 2 tablespoons lemon juice, coriander, oregano, and allspice, and bring to a boil over medium-high heat. Reduce heat to a simmer, cover, and cook about 20 minutes until chicken is tender and juices run clear when flesh is pierced with a fork.
10. While chicken is simmering, prepare scallions, coriander, and pimientos.
11. Transfer chicken to platter and cover loosely with foil. For sauce, add remaining lemon juice and rind to liquid in casserole and stir to combine. Bring to a boil over high heat, and reduce liquid by half, 5 to 8 minutes. Season with salt and pepper to taste.
12. Transfer chicken to individual plates and top each serving with sauce. Sprinkle with scallions, coriander, and pimiento strips and serve garnished with lemon slices.

Margaret Shakespeare

Margaret Shakespeare combines her love of travel with a passion for Mexican food. "Whenever I am in Mexico—at least twice a year—I go to kitchens and restaurants to collect recipes from every cook I can find," she says. Although she feels authentic ingredients are worth seeking out, this cook does not hesitate to substitute more familiar ingredients, even easier methods, to benefit American cooks. For example, in Menu 1, she calls for *mole poblano*, one of the most famous of all the various spicy Mexican *moles*. *Moles* are complex, chili-based sauces, often with as many as twenty ingredients that require day-long cooking (some, even longer). Margaret Shakespeare pares down the ingredient list, and, instead of simmering the chicken in the *mole*, she poaches strips of chicken breast in stock while the sauce cooks separately.

Her other two menus also include classic Mexican dishes. Menu 2 features *huevos rancheros* (ranch-style eggs), a light meal for any time of day. In Menu 3, the hominy soup, or *pozole*, from Guadalajara, is more stew than soup. Traditionally, the meat in this recipe is pig's head, but other versions include pork loin, pig's feet, and chicken. Here, you use lean, boneless pork and chicken thighs. Open-faced bean sandwiches and a salad accompany the soup.

The mole poblano in the casserole is topped with slivered almonds and accompanied by rice with artichoke hearts and a red bell pepper garnish. The mango salad, sprinkled with grated coconut and arranged on a bed of red-leaf lettuce, should be dressed at serving time.

Chicken Mole Poblano
Rice with Artichoke Hearts
Mango Salad

Because the recipe for the sauce is complex, read the directions first and have all your ingredients assembled beforehand. Like many but not all *moles*, this one contains chocolate, yet it is hot, spicy, and only slightly sweet. Taste the sauce before adding the optional sugar (step 10), then add any extra sugar in small amounts.

WHAT TO DRINK

Try a chilled bottle of California or Alsatian Gewürztraminer with this menu.

SHOPPING LIST AND STAPLES

4 chicken breasts, boned, skinned, and split (about
    1½ pounds total weight boned)
Small head red or green leaf lettuce, or small head
    Boston lettuce
Small red bell pepper (optional)
2 medium-size onions
4 cloves garlic
Small bunch parsley
Small bunch coriander (optional)
2 medium-size mangos (1 to 1½ pounds total weight)
Small fresh coconut, or 6-ounce package dried,
    unsweetened
2 limes
1 lemon
1 tablespoon unsalted butter
9-ounce package frozen artichoke hearts, or 14-ounce
    can, water-packed
4-ounce can tomato purée
6 to 7 cups chicken stock, preferably homemade
    (see page 13), or canned
1 tablespoon peanut or safflower oil
1 tablespoon honey
1 package fresh or frozen corn tortillas
1½ cups long-grain rice
2 ounces Mexican chocolate, preferably, or substitute
    (see page 13)
3 tablespoons sugar (optional)
10 dried chilies (4 anchos, 4 mulatos, and 2 pasillas)
    preferably, or 1 tablespoon pure chili powder,
    1½ teaspoons paprika, and 1 teaspoon Cayenne
1 teaspoon ground cinnamon, approximately
½ teaspoon ground cloves, approximately
9-ounce box dark raisins

2 tablespoons hulled sesame seeds
2½-ounce bag blanched almonds
3-ounce jar pine nuts, or 3-ounce can chopped walnuts

UTENSILS

Food processor or blender
2 large saucepans, one with cover
Medium-size saucepan with cover
Small saucepan
Platter
2 small bowls
Colander
Salad spinner (optional)
Measuring cups and spoons
Chef's knife
Paring knife
Wooden spoon
Fork
Rubber spatula
Nut grinder (optional)
Juicer (optional)
Vegetable peeler (optional)

START-TO-FINISH STEPS

One hour ahead: If using frozen tortilla for mole, set out to thaw.

1. Juice lemon and limes for rice and salad recipes. Peel and chop onions for mole and rice recipes.
2. Follow mole recipe steps 1 through 10.
3. While mole sauce is simmering, follow rice recipe steps 1 through 4.
4. While rice is cooking, follow salad recipe steps 1 through 3 and mole recipe steps 11 and 12.
5. When chicken is cooked, follow mole recipe step 13 and rice recipe step 5.
6. Follow salad recipe steps 4 and 5, mole recipe step 14, rice recipe step 6, and serve.

RECIPES

Chicken Mole Poblano

10 dried chilies (4 anchos, 4 mulatos, and 2 pasillas)
    preferably, or 1 tablespoon pure chili powder,
    1½ teaspoons paprika, and 1 teaspoon Cayenne

3 to 4 cups chicken stock, preferably homemade
(see page 13), or canned
¼ cup dark raisins
4 cloves garlic
2 teaspoons chopped coriander for garnish (optional)
¼ cup blanched almonds, plus ½ cup for garnish
(optional)
1 tablespoon peanut or safflower oil
1 fresh or frozen corn tortilla
2 tablespoons hulled sesame seeds
½ to ⅔ cup chopped onion
½ cup tomato purée
2 ounces Mexican chocolate, or substitute (see page 13)
1 teaspoon ground cinnamon, approximately
½ teaspoon ground cloves, approximately
3 tablespoons sugar (optional)
4 chicken breasts, boned, skinned, and split (about 1½
pounds total weight boned)

1. If using dried chilies, bring 4 cups stock to a boil in large saucepan over high heat; if using chili powder, paprika, and Cayenne, bring 3 cups to a boil.
2. While stock is heating, if using dried chilies, prepare them (see page 10) and set aside.
3. If using dried chilies, place them in small bowl and cover them with 1 cup hot stock. In another small bowl, combine raisins with ¼ cup hot stock. Remove pan from heat and reserve stock.
4. Peel garlic and chop coarsely. Wash, pat dry, and chop coriander for garnish, if using. Set aside.
5. In food processor fitted with metal blade, with blender, or with grinder, grind ¼ cup almonds; with chef's knife, sliver remainder, if using. Set aside.
6. In another large saucepan, heat oil over medium heat 20 seconds, or until it shimmers. Tear tortilla into coarse pieces and add to oil. Add sesame seeds and ground almonds, and cook, stirring continuously, about 1 minute, or until mixture is browned.
7. With rubber spatula, scrape mixture into food processor fitted with metal blade or into blender. Add ½ cup hot stock and purée 1 minute.
8. Add soaked chili pieces or chili powder, paprika, and Cayenne, and purée another minute.
9. Add soaked raisins, chopped onion and garlic, and tomato purée, and continue puréeing about 1 minute, or until sauce is thick and almost smooth. (Add a little stock, if necessary, to keep appliance from stalling.) Set aside.
10. With paper towel, wipe saucepan. Scrape sauce into pan and set over low heat. Break chocolate into coarse pieces. Add chocolate, cinnamon, and cloves to taste, and sugar, if using, and stir continuously until chocolate has melted. Simmer, uncovered, about 20 minutes, or until sauce has thickened.
11. Return reserved stock to a boil over medium heat.
12. While stock is heating, cut chicken breasts into strips 2 inches long and ½ inch wide. Add chicken strips to stock, reduce heat, and simmer, uncovered, 15 minutes, or until chicken strips are white and cooked through.

13. Turn chicken strips and remaining stock into sauce and stir until blended. Return to a simmer, cover, and remove pan from heat.
14. Turn chicken mole into serving dish and garnish with slivered almonds and chopped coriander, if desired.

Rice with Artichoke Hearts

9-ounce package frozen artichoke hearts, or
14-ounce can, water-packed
Small red bell pepper for garnish (optional)
3 cups chicken stock
1 tablespoon unsalted butter
¼ cup finely chopped onion
2 tablespoons chopped parsley
1½ cups long-grain rice
2 tablespoons lime juice

1. If using frozen artichoke hearts, separate but do not thaw; if using canned, drain. Cut into quarters. Wash, core, seed, and dice red bell pepper for garnish, if using. Set aside.
2. In small saucepan, bring stock to a boil over medium heat.
3. In medium-size saucepan, melt butter over medium heat. Add onion and parsley, and sauté, stirring frequently, about 2 to 3 minutes, or until onion is translucent. Reduce heat to low.
4. Add rice and stir well to coat with butter. Fold in artichoke hearts. Add lime juice and boiling stock, cover and cook 18 to 20 minutes, or until cooking liquid has been completely absorbed and rice is tender.
5. Remove pan from heat and keep covered until ready to serve.
6. Just before serving, fluff with fork, turn into bowl, and, garnish with chopped red bell pepper, if desired.

Mango Salad

6 to 8 leaves red or green leaf lettuce, or Boston lettuce
2 medium-size mangos (1 to 1½ pounds total weight)
2 tablespoons pine nuts or chopped walnuts
2 tablespoons grated fresh coconut, or dried,
unsweetened
¼ cup lime juice
¼ cup lemon juice
1 tablespoon honey

1. Wash lettuce leaves and dry in salad spinner or pat dry with paper towels. Arrange on serving platter.
2. Peel and pit mangos; cut lengthwise into ½- to ¾-inch-thick slices. Set aside.
3. Arrange mango slices on lettuce leaves and sprinkle with pine nuts or chopped walnuts. Cover with plastic wrap and place in freezer for 15 minutes only.
4. In small bowl, combine coconut, lime and lemon juices, and honey; beat with fork to blend.
5. Remove platter from freezer and pour dressing over salad.

Huevos Rancheros with Salsa Ranchera
Cauliflower Salad
Zucchini-Stuffed Chilies

The *salsa ranchera* (a country-style sauce of tomatoes and fresh chilies) for the *huevos* can be made hotter with extra chilies. Substitute serranos for the jalapeños or combine the two.

When you stuff the *poblano* chilies, leave the stems on to retain the shape. For a more traditional chili dish, coat each stuffed chili with an egg-and-flour batter, then deep fry it in oil. If *poblanos* are not available, use green bell peppers. Blister and skin them (see page 9), retaining the tops but discarding the seeds and membranes.

Each helping of ranch-style eggs on corn tortillas is topped with salsa ranchera *and accompanied by a chili stuffed with an herbed grated zucchini and cheese mixture. Serve the cauliflower salad with the main course.*

WHAT TO DRINK

This brunch or light supper classic suggests another classic: the Bloody Mary. Or try a Bloody Maria, using tequila instead of vodka. Mexican coffee is a good follow-up to the meal.

SHOPPING LIST AND STAPLES

Medium-size head cauliflower (about 1¾ pounds)
3 large ripe tomatoes (about 1½ pounds total weight)
2 medium-size zucchini (about 1 pound total weight)
Small head leafy green lettuce, such as Romaine
4 fresh jalapeños or other hot fresh green chilies,
   or 4-ounce can

4 whole poblano chilies or green bell peppers
2 medium-size white onions
Large red onion
12 cloves garlic
Medium-size bunch fresh parsley
Small bunch fresh dill, or 1 teaspoon dried
1 lime
8 large eggs
½ pint sour cream
¼ pound queso fresco, Monterey Jack, or mild Cheddar
   cheese
4 fresh corn tortillas, 4 inches in diameter, or
   1 package frozen
3-ounce jar Spanish olives stuffed with pimiento
2 cups vegetable oil, approximately

¼ cup plus 2 tablespoons olive oil
2 tablespoons peanut oil
½ teaspoon Dijon mustard
3 tablespoons white wine vinegar
1 tablespoon ground coriander
½ teaspoon chili powder
1 teaspoon oregano
Salt and freshly ground white pepper

UTENSILS

Food processor (optional)
Large skillet
Medium-size skillet or saucepan with cover
2 medium-size saucepans

Platter
Large plate
Salad bowl
Small mixing bowl
Colander
Salad spinner (optional)
Measuring cups and spoons
Chef's knife
Paring knife
Wooden spoon
Metal spatula
Grater (optional)
Juicer (optional)
Whisk
Tongs
Vegetable peeler (optional)

START-TO-FINISH STEPS

One hour ahead: If using frozen tortillas for huevos recipe, set out to thaw.

Thirty minutes ahead: Prepare chilies for salsa and stuffed chilies recipes (see pages 9, 10).

1. Follow salsa recipe step 1.
2. While water for tomatoes is heating, peel and chop white onions; peel and slice red onion; and peel and finely chop garlic. Juice lime. Wash fresh parsley and dill, if using; pat dry and chop coarsely.
3. Follow salsa recipe steps 2 through 5 and salad recipe step 1.
4. Follow stuffed chilies recipe steps 1 through 3.
5. Follow salad recipe steps 2 through 8.
6. Follow salsa recipe step 6.
7. Follow stuffed chilies recipe steps 4 through 8.
8. Follow huevos recipe steps 1 through 5.
9. While eggs are frying, follow salad recipe step 9.
10. Follow huevos recipe step 6, stuffed chilies recipe step 9, and serve with cauliflower salad.

RECIPES

Huevos Rancheros with Salsa Ranchera

2 cups vegetable oil, approximately
4 fresh corn tortillas, 4 inches in diameter, or
   4 frozen tortillas, thawed

8 large eggs
Salsa Ranchera (see following recipe)

1. Fill large skillet one-half-inch full with oil and heat over medium heat until oil shimmers.
2. Line platter with paper towels.
3. Add tortillas to hot oil and fry 1 to 2 minutes, turning once with tongs, until crisp and golden. Transfer to paper-towel-lined platter.
4. Carefully pour off most of oil and reserve. Return skillet to heat and gently break 4 eggs into it. Fry eggs just until set, without turning, or "sunny-side up," adding more oil to skillet if necessary.
5. Place 1 tortilla on each of 4 plates. With spatula, transfer eggs from skillet, arranging 2 on each of 2 tortillas. Repeat with remaining 4 eggs.
6. Spoon some salsa ranchera over eggs and tortillas. Serve additional salsa separately.

Salsa Ranchera

3 large ripe tomatoes (about 1½ pounds, total weight)
2 tablespoons peanut oil
1 cup finely chopped white onion
1 tablespoon chopped garlic
4 fresh jalapeños or other hot fresh green chilies,
   roasted, peeled, and seeded, or 4-ounce can, rinsed,
   patted dry, and seeded

1. Bring 1½ quarts of water to a boil over high heat.
2. Blanch tomatoes 20 to 30 seconds. Transfer to colander and refresh under cold running water; remove peel. In food processor or with chef's knife, chop finely.
3. In same saucepan, heat oil over medium heat. Add onion and garlic, and sauté, stirring with wooden spoon, 4 to 5 minutes, or until onion is translucent.
4. Chop jalapeños, add to mixture, and sauté, stirring continuously, 2 to 3 minutes, or just until tender.
5. Add tomatoes and simmer, stirring occasionally, about 20 minutes, or until sauce is thick.
6. Remove sauce from heat and, stirring occasionally, let cool to room temperature.

Cauliflower Salad

Salt
Medium-size head cauliflower (about 1¾ pounds)
Small head leafy green lettuce, such as Romaine

¾ cup Spanish olives stuffed with pimiento
¼ cup olive oil
3 tablespoons white wine vinegar
1 tablespoon freshly squeezed lime juice
1 tablespoon fresh chopped dill, or 1 teaspoon dried
1 tablespoon ground coriander
½ teaspoon chili powder
½ teaspoon Dijon mustard
1 tablespoon minced garlic
Freshly ground white pepper
1 cup thinly sliced red onion rings, approximately
⅓ cup chopped fresh parsley

1. Bring 1½ quarts of salted water to a boil over medium heat.
2. Break cauliflower into florets and wash thoroughly in colander under cold running water.
3. Add florets to boiling water and cook 8 to 10 minutes, or until tender but still crisp.
4. Wash lettuce and dry in salad spinner or pat dry with paper towels. Tear into bite-size pieces. Set aside.
5. Slice olives lengthwise. Set aside.
6. Turn florets into colander, refresh with cold running water, drain, and let cool.
7. In small mixing bowl, whisk together olive oil, vinegar, lime juice, dill, coriander, chili powder, mustard, and garlic. Season dressing with salt and pepper to taste. Set aside.
8. In salad bowl, combine cauliflower, lettuce, onion, and olives. Cover with plastic wrap and refrigerate until ready to serve.
9. Just before serving, add chopped parsley to salad dressing and stir to recombine. Pour dressing over salad and toss gently.

Zucchini-Stuffed Chilies

2 medium-size zucchini (about 1 pound total weight)
2 tablespoons olive oil
½ cup finely chopped white onion
2 tablespoons chopped garlic
4 ounces queso fresco, Monterey Jack, or
   mild Cheddar cheese
1 teaspoon oregano
1 tablespoon chopped fresh dill, or 1 teaspoon dried
Salt and freshly ground white pepper
⅓ cup sour cream
1 tablespoon freshly squeezed lime juice

4 whole poblano chilies or green bell peppers, roasted, peeled, and seeded

1. Wash, pat dry, and trim zucchini. In food processor fitted with shredding disk or with grater, grate and set aside.
2. In medium-size skillet or saucepan, heat oil over medium heat. Add onion and garlic, and sauté, stirring, 2 to 3 minutes, or until onion is translucent.
3. Stir in grated zucchini, cover, reduce heat to low, and cook, stirring occasionally, about 15 minutes, or until very soft.
4. Crumble cheese, if using queso fresco, or grate. Set aside.
5. Remove cover from zucchini, increase heat to medium-high, and cook about 1 minute, or until liquid has almost evaporated.
6. Stir in cheese, oregano, and dill. Add salt and pepper to taste, reduce heat to medium, and cook about 1 minute, or until cheese melts.
7. Stir in sour cream and lime juice, and cook another 1 to 2 minutes, or until excess liquid has been reduced. Remove pan from heat.
8. Stuff each prepared chili with zucchini mixture. Transfer to large plate, loosely cover, and keep warm on stove top.
9. When ready to serve, transfer chilies to individual plates.

ADDED TOUCH

Piloncillo, the first-choice sweetener for the coffee, is unrefined sugar that has been molded into a solid cone shape. This sugar, available in Mexican groceries and some well-stocked supermarkets, has a molasses-like taste. Grate the cone with a knife or cheese grater.

Mexican Coffee

⅓ cup piloncillo, or brown sugar
Three 3-inch-long cinnamon sticks
½ cup coffee, preferably dark roasted, drip grind

1. In medium-size saucepan, bring 6 cups water, piloncillo, and cinnamon sticks to a boil. Reduce heat and simmer about 15 minutes.
2. Place coffee in filter cone or drip coffee maker. Pour boiling mixture through filter.
3. Serve coffee steaming hot.

Hominy Soup with Salsa Cruda
Mexican Bean-Filled Rolls
Beet and Apple Salad

For this casual meal, serve the hominy soup, topped with some of the salsa cruda and fresh vegetables, in a large tureen. For visual appeal, arrange the bean-filled rolls on a platter and offer the colorful salad on a pottery plate.

Hominy, which is corn kernels without the hull germ, comes in cans in most supermarkets. Look for it in the section with canned beans, where you might also find the canned refried beans for the filled rolls, or *molletes*. Buy a lean cut of pork for this soup, preferably loin. The garnishes are not merely decorative. The soup will taste better with at least two or three of them.

The beet and apple salad, traditionally served in Mexico for Christmas Eve, also is good with sectioned oranges, sliced bananas, or pineapple chunks instead of, or in addition to, the apples.

WHAT TO DRINK

Serve a straightforward, hearty wine such as a Côtes du Rhône or a young Chianti, or, if you prefer beer, try one of the many light-colored, light-bodied ales.

SHOPPING LIST AND STAPLES

1 pound lean boneless pork, cut into ¾-inch cubes
4 chicken thighs (about 1 pound total weight)
Small head cabbage (about ½ pound)
Small bunch radishes
Small bunch red or green leaf lettuce
2 ripe tomatoes (about ¾ pound total weight)
3 jalapeños or other hot fresh chilies, or 4-ounce can
2 medium-size onions
Small bunch scallions
6 cloves garlic
Small bunch coriander
2 medium-size tart apples (about ½ pound total weight)
4 limes
½ pound Chihuahua or Monterey Jack cheese
16-ounce can white hominy
16-ounce can refried beans
16-ounce can or jar water-packed beets
7 tablespoons safflower oil
¼ cup cider or wine vinegar
2 teaspoons Dijon mustard
4 French rolls, or other hard rolls
1 teaspoon sugar
3-ounce jar pine nuts (optional)
9-ounce package raisins (optional)
¼ cup dried oregano, approximately
1 teaspoon ground cinnamon
½ teaspoon ground cardamom

Salt
Whole black peppercorns

UTENSILS

Food processor or blender
Large saucepan with cover
Medium-size saucepan
11 x 17-inch baking sheet (optional)
Platter
2 medium-size bowls
2 small mixing bowls
Colander
Salad spinner (optional)
Measuring cups and spoons
Chef's knife
Bread knife (serrated)
Paring knife
Slotted spoon
Wooden spoon
Metal spatula
Small fork
Cheese grater (optional)
Juicer (optional)
Whisk
Apple corer (optional)

START-TO-FINISH STEPS

Thirty minutes ahead: Prepare chilies for salsa recipe (see pages 9, 10).

1. Follow soup recipe steps 1 through 4.
2. While pork and chicken are cooking, juice limes for salsa and for salad. Follow salsa recipe steps 1 through 3 and salad recipe steps 1 through 8.
3. Follow soup recipe steps 5 through 7.
4. Follow rolls recipe steps 1 through 6.
5. While rolls are broiling, follow soup recipe steps 8 and 9, and salad recipe step 9.
6. Follow rolls recipe step 7 and serve with soup and salad.

RECIPES

Hominy Soup with Salsa Cruda

4 chicken thighs (about 1 pound total weight)
1½ medium-size onions

4 cloves garlic
1 tablespoon safflower oil
1 pound lean boneless pork, cut in ¾-inch cubes
1 teaspoon salt, approximately
¼ teaspoon whole black peppercorns
16-ounce can white hominy
Small head cabbage for garnish
1 cup chopped scallions for garnish
6 to 8 radishes for garnish
2 limes for garnish
Salsa Cruda (see following recipe)
3 to 4 tablespoons dried oregano for garnish

1. Skin chicken thighs. Peel and quarter onions. Peel and halve garlic cloves.
2. In medium-size saucepan, bring 1½ cups water to a boil over medium heat.
3. While water is heating, heat 1 tablespoon oil in large saucepan. Over medium-high heat, add pork cubes and brown, stirring frequently, 5 to 7 minutes, or until cubes are evenly browned.
4. Pour boiling water into saucepan with pork and stir in salt. Add chicken thighs, onions, garlic, and peppercorns. Stir, reduce heat, cover pan, and simmer 30 minutes, or until chicken is tender.
5. With slotted spoon, transfer chicken to medium-size bowl and set aside.
6. Rinse and drain hominy. Stir into soup, cover pan, and simmer another 20 minutes.
7. While hominy is cooking, prepare garnishes for soup: Rinse cabbage and discard any tough, discolored outer leaves; in food processor fitted with shredding disk or with grater, shred. Trim scallions (also for rolls recipe, if desired) and radishes, wash, pat dry, and slice. Rinse limes, pat dry, and slice.
8. Return chicken to soup and add salt to taste.
9. Transfer soup to tureen and decorate with some garnishes, including a dollop of salsa cruda. Serve remaining garnishes and salsa cruda in separate bowls.

Salsa Cruda

3 jalapeños or other fresh hot chilies, roasted, peeled, and seeded, or 3 canned chilies, rinsed, patted dry, and seeded
2 ripe tomatoes (about ¾ pound total weight)
3 tablespoons chopped coriander
½ cup chopped onion
1 teaspoon dried oregano
1 teaspoon freshly squeezed lime juice

1. Chop prepared chilies finely. Wash tomatoes and coriander, pat dry, and chop coarsely.
2. In food processor fitted with metal blade or in blender, combine chilies, tomatoes, onion, coriander, oregano, and lime juice. Chop finely but do not purée. (If using blender, chop by turning blender on and off until desired consistency is reached.)
3. Transfer sauce to serving bowl and set aside.

Mexican Bean-Filled Rolls

4 French rolls, or other hard rolls
½ pound Chihuahua or Monterey Jack cheese
16-ounce can refried beans
½ cup sliced scallions for garnish (optional)

1. Preheat broiler and place rack 4 inches from heating element.
2. With bread knife, slice rolls in half lengthwise. Scoop out soft inside, leaving only the crust as a shell. Reserve soft bread to make bread crumbs for another recipe.
3. Slice or grate cheese.
4. Turn refried beans into small mixing bowl and, with fork, beat briefly.
5. Spoon refried beans into hollowed-out rolls and generously top each half with cheese.
6. Place rolls on baking sheet or foil and broil 5 to 8 minutes, or until bread is crisp and cheese is melted and bubbly.
7. With spatula, transfer rolls to serving platter. Garnish with sliced scallions, if desired.

Beet and Apple Salad

2 medium-size tart apples (about ½ pound total weight)
¼ cup freshly squeezed lime juice
6 to 8 leaves red or green leaf lettuce
16-ounce can or jar water-packed beets
6 tablespoons safflower oil
¼ cup cider or wine vinegar
1 tablespoon crushed garlic
2 teaspoons Dijon mustard
1 teaspoon ground cinnamon
½ teaspoon ground cardamom
1 teaspoon sugar
2 tablespoons pine nuts (optional)
¼ cup raisins (optional)

1. Wash and core apples, but do not peel. Cut into ½-inch dice and place in medium-size bowl. Toss with lime juice, and set aside.
2. Wash lettuce leaves and dry in salad spinner or pat dry with paper towels. Arrange on serving platter.
3. In colander, rinse beets under cold running water, drain, and pat dry with paper towels. Slice and set aside.
4. In small bowl, combine safflower oil, vinegar, garlic, mustard, cinnamon, cardamom, and sugar, and whisk until thoroughly blended. Spoon about half of dressing over lettuce and toss until evenly coated.
5. Drain apples, reserving lime juice, and set aside.
6. Add lime juice to remaining dressing and whisk until blended. Set aside.
7. Arrange a ring of beet slices on the lettuce-lined platter and mound apples in center.
8. Cover salad and chill 30 minutes, or until ready to serve.
9. Just before serving, whisk dressing to recombine and pour over beets and apples. Sprinkle salad with pine nuts and raisins, if desired.

Acknowledgments

Special thanks are due Billie Bledsoe of the *San Antonio Express* and Ann Griswold of the *Houston Chronicle* for their assistance in the preparation of this volume.

The Editors would also like to thank the following for their courtesy in lending items for photography: *Cover*: platters—Dan Bleier, courtesy of Creative Resources; cloth—Pan American Phoenix. *Frontispiece*: wooden spoons, rug—Bowl & Board; tiles—Elon, Inc.; pinch pots—Ann Ruthven; plate—Mark Anderson. *Pages 18–19*: glasses—Conrans; dishes—Gorky Gonzalez, courtesy of Amigo Country, Brooklyn, NY; vase, table, chair—Amigo Country. *Page 22*: glass, tablecloth—Conrans; bowl, plates—Rose Gong; napkin—Marimekko. *Page 24*: bowls, rug—Amigo Country. *Pages 26–27*: flatware—Haviland Limoges; plates—Dan Bleier, courtesy of Creative Resources; tablecloth—Four Hands Bindery; napkin—Leacock & Company. *Pages 30–31*: flatware—The Lauffer Company; glass—Conrans; cloth—Primitive Artisans. *Page 33*: spoon, rug, bowl—Bowl & Board. *Pages 36–37*: flatware—Wallace Silversmiths; glasses, dishes, napkin rings—Haviland Limoges; napkins—Leacock & Company; service plates—Conrans. *Page 40*: flatware—Wolfman-Gold and Good Company; mug—Conrans; dishes, tablecloth—Pan American

Phoenix. *Page 42*: servers—Dean & DeLuca; large bowl—Julien Mousa-Oghli; pie plate, small bowl, tablecloth—Conrans; napkin—Leacock & Company. *Pages 44–45*: flatware—L. L. Bean; glasses, napkins—Conrans; dishes—Columbus Avenue General Store, NYC; tiles—Elon, Inc. *Page 48*: white platters—Buffalo China, Inc.; baskets—Be Seated, Inc.; napkins—Pottery Barn; terracotta plate—Conrans; tiles—Amaru's Tile Selections; round plate—Ann Ruthven; serving spoon—Ad Hoc Housewares. *Page 51*: countertop—Formica® Brand Laminate by Formica Corp.; flatware—Wallace Silversmiths; plates—Patrick Loughran Ceramics; napkin Leacock & Company. *Pages 54–55*: flatware—L. L. Bean; dishes—Mark Anderson. *Page 58*: leather mat—The Tulip Tree Collection, New Milford, CT. *Page 61*: platters, leather—Terrafirma. *Pages 64–65*: straw mat, cloth—Folklorica Imports, Inc.; large bowl, platter, pitcher, ladle—Deruta of Italy, Co.; small bowl—Dan Bleier, courtesy of Creative Resources. *Page 68*: flatware—Wallace Silversmiths; dishes—Ann Ruthven; napkins—Conrans; tablecloth–Brunschwig & Fils. *Page 70*: flatware—Wallace Silversmiths; dishes—Dan Bleier, courtesy of Creative Resources; table—Four Hands Bindery; napkin—Leacock & Company. *Pages 72–73*: flatware—The Lauffer Company; marble

board and bowl, plates, large basket, pitcher, skillet—Pottery Barn; napkins, blanket—Ad Hoc Softwares; tiles—Terra Design, Inc., Morristown, NJ. *Pages 76–77*: flatware—Wallace Silversmiths; dishes—Beth Forer; napkins—Ad Hoc Softwares; tablecloth—Leacock & Company. *Page 79*: dishes—Dan Levy, courtesy of Frank McIntosh at Henri Bendel; rug—Bowl & Board. *Pages 82–83*: plates—Fitz & Floyd. *Page 86*: servers—Robert Murray; casserole, fruit bowl—Rubel & Co.; lace cloth—Ad Hoc Softwares. *Pages 92–93*: small bowl, ladle, green napkin, glasses—Conrans; plates—Buffalo China, Inc.; casserole—Copco; platter—Amigo Country; yellow napkin—Pottery Barn. *Pages 96–97*: flatware, plates—Frank McIntosh at Henri Bendel; bowl, blanket—Bowl & Board. *Page 100*: salad servers—Dean & DeLuca; plates—Mark Anderson; napkin—Frank McIntosh at Henri Bendel; round platter—Conrans; tureen, bowl, long platter—Mad Monk, NY. *Kitchen equipment courtesy of*: White-Westinghouse, Commercial Aluminum Cookware Co., Robot-Coupe, Caloric, Kitchen-Aid, J. A. Henckels Zwillingswerk, Inc., and Schwabel Corp. Microwave oven compliments of Litton Microwave Cooking Products.

Illustrations by Ray Skibinski
Production by Giga Communications

Mail-Order Sources of Mexican Ingredients

Bueno Mexican Foods
P.O. Box 293
Albuquerque, NM 87103
(505) 243–2722

Cardullo's Gourmet Shop
6 Brattle Street
Cambridge, MA 02138
(617) 491–8888

Casa Esteiro
2719 West Division
Chicago, IL 60622
(312) 252–5432

Casa Moneo
210 West 14th Street
New York, NY 10011
(212) 929–1644

Central Grocery Co.
923 Decatur Street
New Orleans, LA 70116
(504) 523–1620

Conte Di Savoia
555 West Roosevelt Road
Chicago, IL 60607
(312) 666–3471

H. Roth and Son
1577 First Avenue, Box F
New York, NY 10028
(212) 734–1110

Index

Time-Life Books Inc. offers a wide
range of fine recordings, including
a Big Band series. For subscription
information, call 1-800-621-7026, or
write TIME-LIFE MUSIC, Time & Life
Building, Chicago, Illinois 60611.